Icarus over the Humber

The Last Flight of Airship R.38/ZR-2

Tom Jamison

LAMPADA PRESS

Icarus over the Humber

The Last Flight of Airship R.38/ZR-2

Tom Jamison

To escape from Crete, Daedalus made wings of feathers and wax for himself and his son Icarus. Disobeying his father's instructions, Icarus flew too close to the sun; the wax melted and he fell to his death.

Le ciel fut son désir, la mer son sépulture:
Est-il plus beau dessein ou plus riche tombeau?

Philippe Destouches

© Tom Jamison

British Library Cataloguing in Publication Data

A catalogue record for this book is available from the British Library.

ISBN 1 873811 03 9

Phototypeset in 11 on 12pt Palatino by Gem DTP, 37 Hunter Road, Elloughton, Brough, HU15 1LG and printed by the Central Print Unit, The University of Hull.

Contents

Dedicated to
Kathleen Gurowich (née Appelbe)
and
William Joy
who were there
and whose memories
of the Howden airship community
inspired this story.

Foreword and Acknowledgements

It was the custom at the former Kingston upon Hull College of Education (Principal: Dr Cyril Bibby) for each tutor to organise an educational project for a group of student teachers during two weeks following the summer terminal examinations. For four years from 1970 I was thus able, with their help, to investigate the largely neglected history of airships in Yorkshire. The idea had been suggested by airship enthusiast Tom Field of Nantwich, who had noticed this gap in the rather arcane chronicles of lighter-than-air aviation.

During my subsequent twenty years of intermittent research I have been helped by a great many people - participants, witnesses, historians, collectors and custodians of material - and I hope that this account of a main event in the Yorkshire airship story will to some extent repay their generosity. When the airships and their people left, they took the available records and their memories with them, and very little evidence remained in local archives of this brief but intense phase of aviation which was centred on Howden Airship Station. To reconstruct the picture it was necessary to locate and reassemble as many fragments of the mosaic as possible, to supplement the press reports which had suffered from wartime censorship and other aberrations. To this end the smallest items could be of value, and I am grateful to everyone who offered memories, material or advice. Sadly, some of them will not see this book.

Special thanks are due to the initial project members, who by their patience and tact encouraged the loan of treasured photographs and artefacts. The first appeal in the John Humber Column of the *Hull Daily Mail* brought a limited response, but as word spread that the interviewers were respectable (this being a time of student turmoil), many more people came forward.

For the ongoing research I am particularly indebted to the following individuals for the dedication of time and material and the unselfish sharing of their resources:- Mr Tom Asquith, MBE; Mr

Charles Ayre; Mr Dennis Burchmore; Mr David Cook and Mr Richard Cook; Mr and Mrs P Faulkner; Mrs Kathleen Gurowich; Mr Dennis Habberfield-Bateman; Mr William Joy; Dr Peter Pritchard and Dr James Pritchard.

While I am grateful to everyone else who has helped to compile the Yorkshire airships story, I ask to be forgiven for listing only those whose evidence has the most direct bearing on the main events from 1916 to 1921, especially the R.38 story:- Mr G Barwick; Mr and Mrs R Batchelor; Mrs Barrett; Mr Baxter; Mr W R Beck; Mr and Mrs Biscombe; Mr G Branton; Mr L Briskham; Mr G R Cade; Mrs Cheeseman; Mr H Constable; Mrs J Craven; Mr and Mrs G F Cooper; Mr Cotton; Mrs Cutsforth; Mr F W Daddy; Mr Dale; W/Cdr W Dunn; Mrs B Farmery; Mr N Forester: Mr F Foster; Miss M Fowler; Mrs D Frearson; Mrs A Gorbert; Mr H Grainger; Mrs M Grindell; Mrs M Grove; Mr T Hancox; Mrs M Hayward; Mr Holmes; Mr Hepworth; Mr A Hewitt; Mr Hodgson; Mr G Hotham; Mrs Lumb; Mrs G Matthews; Mr H C Mowthorpe; Mr G Nicholson; Mr W Robinson; Mrs Savage; Mr F Smith, Mr K Stephenson; Mr N Ulyott; Mr J W Ward; Mrs R E Watkin; Mr L A Whittle; Mr C J Woodisse.

I found the staff of archives, libraries and museums, past and present, to be consistently pleasant, and some individual officers have gone out of their way to be helpful. It seems only fair to name them:- The British Library, Thorp Arch; Bridlington Public Library; Goole Public Library (Miss Thomson, Mr Lawson); Hull Public Libraries (particularly Miss Crowther); Hull Record Office (Mr Oxley); Hull Museums (Mr Credland); Humberside Archive Service (Mr Holt); the former Humber Conservancy Board; Imperial War Museum; Museum of Flight, East Fortune (S/Ldr Major); Public Record Office, Kew; Royal Aeronautical Society (Mr Nayler); Royal Air Force Museum. At the Yorkshire Air Museum, Elvington, the airship displays have attracted a number of new witnesses and donors of material.

The following newspapers and periodicals in public and private collections were searched for contemporary and retrospective material:-

Aeronautical Engineering; The Aeroplane; The Airship; Daily Graphic; Daily Mail; Daily Record (Glasgow); Daily Sketch; The Dalesman; Eastern Morning News; The Engineer; Evening Standard; Flight; Goole Times; Hull Daily Mail; Hull and Yorkshire Times; New York Times; Rosedowns News Bulletin; Selby Times; The Times; Yorkshire Post.

The acknowledgement of illustrations is a problem, as material was duplicated in several collections and often the original source was not known. To avoid offence, may I say that much of the visual content was loaned or donated by individuals who have already been mentioned, and the remainder, with a few exceptions (attributed), have come from the following main sources:-

Asquith Collection; Dawson Collection; Cook Collection; FOCAS (Friends of Cardington Airship Station - recently renamed Airship Heritage Trust); Museum of Flight, East Fortune; Pritchard Collection. I am grateful to Revd Bill Mash for permission to photograph the Elloughton Memorial, and to Mr Arnold Nayler for access to the memorial at the Royal Aeronautical Society.

The vital American connection was made through the kindness of Mrs Margaret Engelhart of Plattsburg, NY, who searched the *New York Times* and also provided contact addresses. Mr Larry Wilson of the Smithsonian Institution located information about the personnel of the Howden Detachment, and Ms Judith Walters of the Naval Historical Center sent CVs of its officers. I am grateful to Mr Vincent L Barile, Ms Laura Drake and Ms Kathy Shenkle of the Department of Veterans Affairs for searching for the burial locations of the United States Naval casualties. The efforts of these individuals are the more welcome because of the difficulty of personal contact.

Two authors in particular helped in the search for the human element: Patrick Abbott, who put me in touch with the Pritchard family; and Peter Connon, whose meticulous attention to detail gives an insight into the lives of the airshipmen.

Conscious of the need for technical accuracy, I gratefully accepted the advice of Mr Norman Peake of Norwich and Mr Stanley Tyacke of Hull regarding the engineering aspects of the disaster, but if there are any residual errors or misinterpretations of the evidence, they are mine alone.

I am impressed by the patience of Messrs Raymond and Alistair Fielden, father and son, who translated my scribbled manuscript into legible print, and accepted the many revisions with good grace. I was fortunate in the later stages to have the expert guidance of Dr Holmes and Miss Jean Smith of The University of Hull Press, who have eliminated my inherent untidiness from the finished book.

A special tribute is due to my wife Elma, who has facilitated and endured the long, eccentric and often tedious pursuit of airship history, in all weathers and many locations.

Tom Jamison   Hull, 1994

List of Illustrations

R.38/ZR-2 at Howden

Introduction

To the east of the Pennines and from the Wash through to the rise of the North York Moors is flat land, drained by slow rivers and spared the worst of the Atlantic weather by the mountain barrier to the west.

The Romans came here, displacing or enslaving the occupants, to safe havens for their ships and fertile land to colonise and to feed their armies. They stayed some time and left traces on landscape and language, agriculture and architecture.

The Danes followed, but they were not great builders, and place-names are the main evidence of their considerable presence, which was effectively terminated by the Black Death.

Next came the Normans. They left castles and monasteries, crumbling now but still evocative of former size and importance and sited where they could benefit from the soil and the rivers and dominate the highways laid down by the Romans.

The abolition of the monasteries brought a new breed of occupier - the *nouveau riche* aristocracy who grabbed the spoils and built their own secular monuments along the north-seeking roads. Many of these stately residences contain stone recycled from forts and abbeys.

There have also been temporary occupiers. Because of its physical and strategic geography, armies have lived and occasionally fought in this gentle country. It was garrisoned by the Romans and Normans; raided and settled by the Danes; defended by King Harold's luckless army; disputed by Roundhead and Cavalier. King William's continental armies passed this way to 'liberate' Ireland. As a potential invasion target it has long been the home to regiments which also fed the campaigns of Britain's Empire. In living memory it has hosted soldiers, sailors and airmen - most numerously in World War II, when Bomber Command made use of the aerodrome-friendly terrain.

So much history has inevitably given rise to the stories of ghostly legionaries and monks and troopers. Stand on an abandoned airfield at dusk and try to disbelieve the reports that the restless shades of airmen are wandering among the ruins!

For the modern visitor, following the A1 or A15 or almost any north bound route, the evidence of this last great occupation subtly emerges from the landscape. An alien patch of paving interrupts a cornfield; a silhouette grows on a skyline. Broken concrete is heaped at the end of the partly healed scar of a former runway; a wartime aircraft hanger serves as a barn: a flying control tower has become a dwelling. Among the trees or in the corner of a field a barrack or ablution block survives as a cattle shelter or implement store, unmistakable by the external buttresses on the single-brick walls. A few solidly built permanent aerodromes lie eerily quiet like enormous deserted film lots awaiting the next production. Forty years of peace have returned the flatlands to rural pursuits or to a new industrial colonisation of the abandoned sites. The remaining acres of concrete may be useful bases for mountains of straw bales or clamps of root crops, but for the sake of the plough the farmer will have planted posts to mark the buried drains, pipes and foundations which are beyond economical removal. This is an archaeological site on a grand scale, for the most part visible only by aerial photography or commemorated in the street names of the new industrial or housing estates; Lancaster Drive, Halifax Road. It was geography that brought the bombers - and fighters and reconnaissance planes in smaller numbers - to this part of England. It was level, not overpopulated, and was as near to a hostile Europe as aerodromes could conveniently be. It also faced the North Sea where coastal shipping had to be protected and where traffic vital to enemies had to be sought and destroyed.

What the traveller will not find, unless guided by foreknowledge or esoteric interest, is an older airfield, hidden by scrub willow and a new municipal golf course. Here was a focal point of British *lighter-than-air* flight between 1915 and 1922. As the testing station for the large *rigid* airships and a base for the smaller anti-submarine *blimps* it was host to almost every type of airship operated by the Royal Naval Air Service and the RAF. It was also the birthplace of Barnes Wallis's incomparable R.100 - built on site between 1926 and 1929.

This was Howden Airship Station. For the sentimental historian (and aren't we all?), Howden and its environs is as good a focus as any to evoke the days of this specialised, romantically archaic branch of aviation. Standing by the overgrown foundation of No.1 Airship shed, it is easy to imagine the comings and goings of the airships and their people and the impact on the local rural community of one thousand servicemen and women - the forerunner of many such arbitrary impositions in a later war. Apart from some dispossessed farmers, it was not bad news for the area, and there were commercial as well as social benefits to be gained. Civilian workers were required to build and service the station, and lodgings were sought by servicemen with living-out passes. It was a sort of symbiosis of mutual support, in which the civil and service elements became an airship community, and proud of it.

The long history of airships has been told many times with varying accuracy, but always with the fascination of a lost cause. This limited account will cover less than twenty years of the story and will aim to evoke the ethos of the British Airship Service in its successes and failures, high hopes and deep disappointments, joy and grief - but above all the family atmosphere of a close-knit community with common purpose and loyalty. Always at the mercy of whimsical policy makers and facing the perils and hardships which are the lot of pioneers, they had a deep pride in and dedication to the cause of lighter-than-air flight. They included not only the airship crews, but the thousands of men and women who built, serviced and handled the giant flying machines and those who provided the ancillary services at the airship stations.

I

Background

Some pre-history and a few basic technicalities may help to set the scene.

In the early years of the 20th Century there was keen rivalry between the proponents of airships, which had already been around with varying success for fifty years, and the enthusiastic aeronauts who were building and using the early flying machines. The Wright Brothers in USA had been narrowly the first in 1903 to achieve the ancient dream of powered flight, but other inventors were already in the field. They were soon joined by a mixed fraternity of backyard designers and well-heeled sportsmen who between them were to develop the new science - with minimal government interest or support. In Britain, clubs and schools were formed and air pageants and itinerant fliers spread the enthusiasm to an eager public, for whom aviation was the last word in spectator sports.

In France, which had seen the beginnings of the science of aerostatics in the balloon flights of the Montgolfier brothers and Professor Charles in 1783, there had been successful demonstrations of *directed* flight by engine driven airships. Most of these early *dirigibles* (navigable balloons) were elongated gasbags supporting a framework which carried the power unit and crew and also the steering devices. Although also seen as sporting novelties, their military potential was obvious - at least to the younger members of the armed services.

In Germany the outstanding pioneer of the lighter-than-air flight was the ageing Count Zeppelin, who by 1914 had demonstrated the safety, comfort and endurance of his rigidly framed airships as passenger carriers. The German High Command had been quick to recognise the scouting and offensive possibilities of the new machines and in spite of accidents both army and navy were developing air arms.

In Britain the Royal Engineers experimented with some small airships and the Royal Navy commissioned a rigid airship on the Zeppelin pattern. Completed in 1911, HM Airship No.1 (nicknamed *Mayfly*), broke its back without ever flying and the project was shelved for the time being. And arms dealers being basically businessmen, it was easy for the Admiralty to purchase a German-designed *Parseval* non-rigid airship immediately prior to the war, with a licence to build further ships to the same pattern.

Thus the situation at the outbreak of the Great War in 1914 was a lead in military *airship* development by Germany while Britain had a pool of expertise (largely amateur and unsponsored) in the science of *aerodynamics* or heavier-than-air flight. This of course is a simplification, as most countries anticipating the war were looking at *all* potential weapons and far-sighted individual officers of all services were keeping an eye on developments. Certain Royal Navy and Army officers had flown as civilian passengers in Count Zeppelin's fine machines. A small number of British officers had also privately learned to fly aeroplanes or balloons, a few enjoying the War Office subsidy of £75 for their lessons. However far-sighted or enthusiastic these individuals were, it required commitment from a government to develop the war potential of a new science and in Britain in 1914 the commitment was largely to conventional land and sea forces. Military aviation was regarded as no more than a means of seeing what the other side was up to and had a low priority for funds or manpower. Although an obvious extension of the scouting role of cavalry, it was resented by the traditionalists who thought it would 'frighten the horses' and poach in their territory. This complacency was shattered in 1915 when the superbly trained but conventional regular British Army suffered a humiliating defeat, largely through failing to think in terms of mobile warfare and having already forgotten the recent lessons of the Anglo-Boer War of 1899-1902.

The inevitable development of aerial *reconnaissance* soon led to *offensive* air operations in all theatres of war, and to a rapid development of aeroplanes. Meanwhile the war on land embedded itself in mud and demanded more and more men and material, giving the British public a very personal interest in the struggle as they were recruited for the services, industry or agriculture. At sea the Royal Navy had not yet had the severe lesson of Jutland and was still regarded as Britain's Sure Shield. However, further nasty surprises were brewing which were to have an impact on British aviation.

The first was the unexpected and terrifying bombing campaign by Zeppelins and other German airships against undefended British towns, which caused some damage and loss of life but was devastating to civilian morale. Guns and men had to be diverted from the 'real' war to fight the 'baby-killers', the main defensive weapons being aeroplanes and anti-aircraft guns. A killer airship was designed but never saw service and most of the Zeppelins destroyed were caught by aircraft. Two which were brought down and salvaged were to have a potent and ultimately tragic influence on British airship design.

The Battle of Jutland in 1916 merely increased the Royal Navy's neurosis about being spied upon from above, as several Zeppelins were present above the battle. Of course this was long before the invention of radar. Their usefulness may have been exaggerated, but they - and the bombing campaign - spurred the British Government into reviving the rigid airship programme, including building of key airship stations around the country, manned by the Royal Naval Air Service (RNAS).

But something even deadlier was happening under the sea. From early 1915 the German submarine campaign was sinking merchant ships at a rate which threatened to starve Britain into submission. In the event, it was a close-run contest, but by a strange irony, the neutral-buoyancy undersea vessel was to be defeated with the help of a neutral-buoyancy flying machine. This is the subject of Chapter 3.

*   *   *

Meanwhile, and without too much technicality, some idea of the construction and operation of airships of the period may be useful.

Basically there were two main types, the *rigid* and the *non-rigid*, and a hybrid *semi-rigid*. Britain possessed only two of the latter - an early experimental model and one bought from Italy in 1918. The rigid airship was immense - the size of an ocean liner - and had a framework of girders covered by fabric. The girders were of aluminium, duralumin or plywood and were braced by steel cables. Inside the frame were a number of fabric gas cells containing *hydrogen*, the lightest of all gases, each enclosed in netting attached to the girders. Engine cars and a navigational *control* car were suspended outside the hull on struts. These appendages were sometimes referred to as *gondolas*. A keel corridor ran the entire length of the airship to provide access to fuel and oil tanks and some very basic accommodation for the crew. At intervals along the keel there were rubberised bags containing ballast water which could be dropped to trim or lighten the ship as required. It was frequently dumped on take off or landing, to the discomfort of the ground landing crews, particularly if it contained glycerine or alcohol as anti-freeze.

Bomb bays were located inside the hull and there could be machine guns on top and in the control and engine cars. Operating such a craft was a giant balancing act, involving not only the lift of the hydrogen and the weight of the ship, crew, fuel, bomb load and ballast, but also atmospheric conditions and the *dynamic* lift which could be obtained from the ship's speed.

Of all these factors, the atmosphere was the most fickle, and imposed constant vigilance on the captain or officer of the watch. The gas cells, made of light cotton lined with goldbeater's skin, were partially filled at ground level to allow for expansion of the hydrogen as the outside air pressure decreased with altitude. Once the bags became fully distended, gas was automatically valved. The airship was then said to be at *pressure height*. This loss of gas (and thereby potential lift) might have to be compensated by dropping ballast on descent to a lower altitude. Superheating of the gas by sunlight increased the lift and might require manual valving to remain at operational height. Conversely rain or cloud would cool the gas, making the ship heavy - in addition to the increased weight of a wet outer cover. In this case, it might require the dropping of ballast to remain airborne. In an emergency some fuel tanks could be 'slipped' by cutting their supporting wires. As a further complication, cold dense air gave more lift than warm air and a ship encountering a warm layer could suddenly lose buoyancy.

Minor fluctuations in lift were adjusted by using the *dynamic lift* in a positive or negative direction by angling the ship's bow up or down by means of the elevators, controlled by the height coxswain. This experienced crewman faced athwartships in order to sense the pitching of the ship, as a large dirigible tended to 'hunt' about a mean track, and to maintain level flight he had to anticipate the control requirements. Unfortunately dynamic flying greatly increased fuel consumption.

There was also a steering cox'n, facing forward, maintaining a magnetic compass course by operating the rudders, and he also had to be sensitive to the wayward tracking of the enormous vessel.

In theory an airship could remain aloft indefinitely or as long as the fuel lasted, but constant adjustments involving gas valving and dropping ballast limited the endurance. Even the consumption of fuel added to the problem, as the reduced weight might dictate valving off gas to compensate. Later on, water recovery systems were used to adjust for the loss of fuel, either by collecting rainwater or by condensing exhaust gases. The Howden built R.100 was probably the first to use the former method.

An experienced pilot would juggle the elements, dodging into cloud to avoid superheating or flying in sunlight if the cover needed drying out.

All this was in addition to the complexities of navigation without the help of radar or reliable meteorological forecasts.

There was one other major problem peculiar to the big rigids. Whereas the crew might number from 14 upwards - depending mainly upon the length and purpose of the flight - up to 500 ground crew could be required for launching and landing.

The *useful load* of a large airship (i.e. gross lift minus weight of structure and fittings) could be as much as 50 tons but was considerably less in the early British ships. Much of the load would be fuel, ballast and crew, leaving little for bombs or defensive armament.

The *non-rigid* or *limp* airship differed substantially in design, purpose, size and operation from its big sister. Also colloquially known as a 'blimp', it was more correctly called a *pressure airship*. Instead of separate cells, the hydrogen was contained in a single envelope of rubberised fabric which was kept in shape by the internal gas pressure - at the surprisingly low manometer pressure of 30mm of water - with bamboo battens to stiffen the bow against air resistance in flight. To compensate for the expansion and contraction of gas due to height and atmospheric conditions two or more ballonets or internal air bags were inflated inside the envelope. By pumping or valving air to and from the ballonets, the relative gas pressure could be maintained, and by shifting air to the forward or rear compartments the trim could be adjusted. For example, more air in the rear and less in the front made the nose lighter. A large scoop behind the propeller collected the air for the ballonets, although some later craft had battery-powered booster pumps. A non-rigid airship which lost the required pressure was a sorry sight and as the control surfaces were carried on the envelope the wilting made it unmanageable and it would have to make a forced landing.

Beneath the envelope, suspended by cables attached to the fabric by various load-distributing methods, the control car or gondola would be slung. In the small ships this also carried the engine. The larger craft had a separate gantry supporting two or more engines. Some classes had petrol tanks slung on or inside the envelope, but the ballast tanks were in the control car, together with bombs, sea markers and machine guns. As their main purpose was maritime patrol, later control cars were designed to float, so that a descent could be made on the water.

They were handy craft, with a crew of from two to ten, depending on their size and intended flight duration. Compared to the 600 or 700 feet length of a rigid, the blimp was a modest 140 to 200 feet. The gas capacity being much less, the useful lift was sufficient only to sustain the crew, fuel and ballast and a few small bombs. Although the range in miles was not great, the endurance was spectacular for its time, and quite adequate for coastal shipping protection. The smallest craft could officially maintain a patrol of at least twelve hours, and the largest twenty one hours. This was often exceeded by a skilled pilot, who would be a very busy man. In addition to navigating he had to be constantly aware of the gas pressure and adjust for the same atmospheric vagaries which bedevilled the big ships. His craft being shorter he would have to endure bumps instead of the slow pitching of the rigids, especially when flying over land to and from patrol.

The *semi-rigid* was essentially a pressure airship with a long keel structure attached to the envelope to give rigidity. Loss of pressure did not have such a devastating effect on the control surfaces, and the weights could be distributed more evenly along the keel instead of being concentrated in the control car.

Launching an airship of any type was generally easier than landing it, as it could be *weighed off* or balanced to the desired buoyancy before take-off. On the command 'Let go' or 'Hands off together' (often by bugle call or whistle) the ground crew would release it or would give an upward push in unison. Some ballast might be dropped, or the engines revved to give dynamic lift. It was possible to take an airship up slightly 'heavy' by the expedient of the ground crew literally throwing it into the air.

On landing, the pilot would choose between descending 'light' under power to place his trail rope and handling guys in the hands of the ground crew, or by valving gas to descend and discharging ballast at the last moment. Understandably, this latter method was not popular among ground crew handlers.

By comparison, the aeroplane of the day was a midget, with limited load and endurance but a greater turn of speed. It was comparatively cheap and easy to produce in quantity, and required much less in the way of ground staff for handling and maintenance. It was also more versatile in attack and defence than the airship, but could not climb as rapidly and lost manoeuverability at high altitudes.

II

The Zeppelins

While the British Admiralty was still dithering about the need for an air arm and had reluctantly commissioned Vickers to build a second rigid airship (HMA No.9; ordered June 1913; cancelled April 1915; reordered June 1915; first flown in November 1916), the German Army and Navy were earnestly training airship crews, and by the end of 1914 both services had several *Luftschiffe* in commission, and others on order from the Zeppelin and Schütte-Lanz Companies. The Army also used Parseval non-rigids, similar to P.4, which had been bought by the Royal Navy just before the war.

Count Zeppelin, an ex-cavalryman, had always thought of airships in terms of scouting and reconnaissance, and this was the way in which they were first used. It soon became obvious that flying over heavily armed troops in daylight was foolhardy, four Army Zeppelins having been shot down during August 1914, the first month of the war. This led to night flying, in which they were more effective for bombing than reconnaissance, and to the realisation that it did great damage to enemy morale - out of all proportion to the weight of bombs dropped.

It was not long before senior officers, backed by German public opinion, were pressing the Kaiser to let them bomb England, where such attacks '. . . may be expected, whether they involve London or the neighbourhood of London, to cause panic in the population which may possibly render it doubtful that the war can be continued'. These words, written by the Deputy Chief of the Naval Staff, show the frustration of the Imperial Navy due to the *Hochseeflotte* being confined to secure harbours by blockade, and unwilling to face the superior resources of the Royal Navy until it could choose its own background.

The German Naval Zeppelins were doing useful work in watching for the approach of British naval raiders, but this was mainly defensive and not nearly so rewarding as dropping bombs on the very heart of the enemy.

Kaiser Wilhelm, Supreme War Lord of both Army and Navy and regarded as a bloodthirsty bogeyman by the Allies, had tender feelings for his cousins in the British Royal Family and some scruples about the danger to historic buildings; and it was not until January 1915 that he was persuaded to sanction attacks on 'docks and military establishments in the lower Thames and on the English coast'. London was not to be bombed west of the Tower, thus ruling out prime targets such as the Stock Exchange, the Bank of England and - most tempting of all - the Admiralty. It was to be several frustrating months before His Imperial Majesty lifted the ban, and London received its first unrestricted raid on the night of 9/10 August 1915.

Although there was intense rivalry between the two airship services, and the Army already had experience of bombing operations, it was the Navy which sent the first Zeppelins against England on 19 January 1915, targeting the River Humber and the Thames. Fregattenkapitän Peter Strasser, the dedicated and forceful leader of the Naval Airship Division, was on board Zeppelin L.6 as an observer for the politically sensitive raid on the Thames, but an engine failure aborted the attempt. L.3 (Kapitänleutnant Fritz) and L.4 (Kplt. Count von Platen-Hallermund) were driven south by the wind, L.3 changing course for Norfolk and L.4 arriving there by default. So it was that Great Yarmouth received the first six 50 Kg explosive bombs and seven incendiaries of the bombing campaign from L.3, causing little damage but killing two civilians.

Von Platen in L.4 was lost, about eighty miles southeast of his target; but having come so far he dropped two incendiaries on the Norfolk village of Snettisham and the remainder of his load on Kings Lynn, where he killed a woman and a boy. Returning to base after the flight of 22 hours and 50 minutes he reported that he had 'successfully bombed fortified places between the Tyne and the Humber'.

This first attempt illustrates two problems experienced by the raiders which were to bring the northeastern coastal areas of England more than their share of attention. The first was the slow speed of the early Zeppelins - a mere 50-60 mph - which put them very much at the mercy of the wind on a long flight, and often dictated the target to head for. It was useless trying for the Thames from northern airship bases such as Tondern, Nordholz or Ahlhorn against a southwesterly wind (the prevailing airstream of the British Isles) and while other winds might hasten the arrival they could delay the return flight and increase the danger of pursuit or interception by aircraft. Calm, cold weather was best for *useful lift* - allowing more fuel for longer range or more bombs to be carried; also, navigation was simpler in light winds. Unfortunately the fickle British weather could reverse the most perfect conditions during a flight of 20 - 24 hours, and winds of unknown strength and direction could upset the most careful route planning.

The second problem - often exacerbated by the weather - was the crudity of aerial navigation in those early days and the lack of suitable maps and other aids. Even the navigation instructors were unsure of their ground (in all senses), as they had been trained to con ships in waters which were properly charted and in which the currents and tides were well known.

A further complication was that the shortest route to London was by flying close to the coast of neutral Holland (in daylight, to arrive at dusk) with the certainty of being reported to the English defenders. As it was not much greater distance to the East Coast ports it was tempting to head directly across the open North Sea, to make landfall on a coast with features such as the Wash, Humber, Tees and Tyne - all of which showed up against the land at night. Midway between the Humber and the Tees there was the prominent Flamborough Head, with lightly defended land on either side to give a good run in to the industrial cities of the Midlands and North. The Holderness Plain, lacking hills, was much favoured as an entry point.

Once the coast had been passed there were few checks on position, and as cloudy and moonless nights were preferred, the captain of a raider might have to bomb any likely but unknown target. His combat report would naturally claim a positive result which would be triumphantly quoted by the German press.

If this uncertainty saved a few prime industrial or military targets, it caused great nervousness among the civilian population and initially came close to causing the general panic which had been predicted by the German High Command. It was not just the distinctive drone of the Maybach engines which sent shivers up the spine as the intruders meandered in search of a target. Ironically, as the defences became more organised the warnings of possible raids came earlier and alerted a wider area. The intelligence came from neutral observers, ships at sea and listening posts in Britain - but increasingly by monitoring *Luftschiffe* wireless telegraphy traffic which gave an early indication of the size and even direction of an attacking force. Warnings would be telephoned to possible target areas and relayed to factories which would sound the alarm by a series of blasts on their hooters (commonly known as 'buzzers'). In Hull the distinctive steam whistle of Blundell's Paint Factory was the major herald of doom. As this could happen early in the day to allow workers to go home, it would put the population into a state of nervous anticipation until the 'all clear' was given by a steady note

Fig. 1 After the raid of 6/7 June 1915 - Edwin Davis's Store destroyed,
but Holy Trinity Church spared. It gave the erroneous idea that Zeppelin bombing
was accurate.

Fig. 2 A number of houses were destroyed in the same raid.

Fig. 3 Zeppelins shot down and salvaged, including L.70 (above) and L.33 (below),
influenced the design of British rigid airships, especially R.38/ZR-2.

Fig. 4 The wreckage of L.33 at Little Wigborough, Essex - one of the grounded
Zeppelins which influenced the design of the British rigids.

on the buzzer. An imminent raid might be signalled by police whistles or by the gunfire (usually futile) of any troops in the area. The most sinister warning at night was the dimming of the street lamps, of which the top halves were already painted blue, by reducing the pressure at the gasworks. This would also dim the lights in many gaslit homes.

Compared with the air raids in World War II, the damage and casualties inflicted by the Zeppelin (and occasional Schütte-Lanz) raiders were comparatively small - a total of 556 killed and 1357 injured in Britain throughout the war - but it was a novel terror, in which the suspense had a very bad effect on morale. There was something horrific and personally threatening about a huge predator slowly and deliberately searching for a target, with the ability to hover when it had found one.

The citizens of Hull and the Humber littoral endured more than two years of this torment, and their experiences and reactions will illustrate the effect on civilian morale of this new form of warfare. For them it commenced with a raid on 6/7 June 1915 by Zeppelin L.9, commanded by Kapitänleutnant Mathy, one of the most determined and successful of the naval airship pilots. Having reached the coast in fog he at last recognised Bridlington and set course for Hull, which he reached at 12.50am. With little opposition, apart from a single small cruiser in dock armed only with a 4 inch gun, he chose his targets carefully, dropping ten explosive and fifty incendiary bombs on docks, a timber yard and Old Town. Edwin Davis's drapery store, beside Hull's ancient Holy Trinity Church, was completely destroyed; the church losing only a few windows. Taken as evidence of accurate bombing, this may have strengthened the belief that the destruction of a number of terrace houses was also deliberate. The damage was estimated at £44,795 - a considerable sum in those days - making it the most cost-effective raid up to that time.

L.9's bombs had killed 24 people and injured another 40, and in a sad but understandable reaction there were immediate attacks on shops with German or German-sounding names. Not content with looting the shops, some rioters invaded homes, carrying off or destroying furniture. There may have been some logic in looting the edible stock of a pork butcher, but for good measure his flat above was ransacked, his windows broken and his piano thrown into the street after the crowd had been treated to *God Save the King* by a patriotic musician. There was some police action and fines were imposed on those caught with looted (presumably inedible) property. Many of the victims lost their livelihood without compensation. Spy fever spread rapidly and accusations were made against persons suspected of having signalled to the raiders - probably only guilty of having opened a curtain at the wrong moment.

Even less logical was the stoning of a Royal Flying Corps motor tender, presumably to show displeasure about the lack of defences.

Thus conditioned by a practical demonstration of Zeppelin terror, the population lived with the possibility that their turn might come again. As the frequency of the attacks built up over the country, there was a nightly exodus from Hull to the apparent safety of green fields, at that time not so far outside the city centre. People slept in open fields at Anlaby, Newland or Sutton, or found what shelter they could under railway arches or in sports pavilions. Had they but known, the protection offered by a rural retreat was illusory as bombs were often released blindly through cloud after the briefest sighting of a town. They might even be jettisoned to lighten ship for the journey home. Many of the raiders on Hull and its environs approached from the west, which suggests that they had failed to find a target inland. The bomb load might also be dumped to speed the ascent if anti-aircraft shells or hostile aeroplanes got too close.

The following list of raids on the Humber area makes the point that there was something real to be afraid of, but also that there was an element of chance about the target selection:-

DATE		BOMBED	KILLED	INJURED
1915	6/7 June	Hull	24	40
	10 August	Goole (in error for Hull)	16	
1916	31 Jan/1 Feb	Scunthorpe (in error for Goole)	3	7
	5 March	Hull and near Beverley (2 raiders)		
	1 April	Cleethorpes (barracks)	29	53
	8/9 August	Hull	10	11
1917	21/22 August	Random bombs east of Hull		1

This does not convey the prolonged anxiety brought on by the frequent overflights to inland targets and the general alerts when raiders were known to be approaching the East Coast, possibly for East Anglia, Hartlepool or Sunderland. However, people are resilient, and the extreme collapse of morale which the High Command had hoped for did not recur after the first unfortunate outbursts. Instead a smouldering resentment built up against the 'baby-killers', so that the flaming destruction of a Zeppelin or

Schütte-Lanz raider had a greater tonic effect than winning a battle. Gradually the defences improved and the provision of searchlights, anti-aircraft guns and night-flying aeroplanes restored public confidence - somewhat shattered in Hull when it was discovered that the gun on Rose, Downs and Thomson's foundry roof was a wooden dummy, though it was never clear whether it was intended to scare the Zeppelins or reassure the population. People would stay out to watch the searchlights sweeping the sky until they caught and coned an intruder, 'looking like a silver cigar', regardless of the rain of hot splinters from anti-aircraft shells or the possibility that the captain might jettison his bomb load to escape upwards.

Typical of the times, an enterprising balladeer wrote new words to the popular tune *Back home in Tennesee* to celebrate the downing of one Zeppelin. Printed on a postcard, it sold for 1d. (one old penny). It commenced:

> His home in Germany, that Zep will never see,
> The British gunnery did bring it down you see.
> All he could think of that night was of setting
> Hull alight . . . etc.

In spite of heavy losses, the raids continued with a few welcome breaks until August 1918, becoming increasingly a Naval effort as the Army had to put all its resources into the land battle. Among the casualties was Heinrich Mathy, who was found embedded in the ground after jumping from the blazing L.31, shot down by Second Lieutenant W. J. Tempest at Potters Bar on 2 October 1916. The loss of this most daring of Zeppelin commanders cast a great gloom over the survivors, but it was good news for Humberside; Mathy had been the bomber of Hull and Goole.

The end came on 5 August 1918 when Peter Strasser, now designated *Führer der Luftschiffe* by order of the Kaiser, led a final desperate sortie by five Zeppelins. His modern *height-climber* L.70 was shot down off Norfolk by Major Egbert Cadbury and Captain Robert Leckie in a DH4 aircraft.

* * *

What then was the overall effect of the first sustained aerial bombardment of a civil population?

Certainly there was material damage, but nothing to compare to the wastage that was going on by land and sea during every day of the Great War. Those who had lost homes and possessions and possibly loved ones faced true hardship, as they had to put their pathetic claims in writing (often with difficulty) to the London-based

East Coast Raid Committee, while doubling up with neighbours or relations or relying on the charity of voluntary organisations.

There were degrees of hardship. Alice Walker lost her husband and two daughters in the first Hull raid when her house in St. Thomas Street was destroyed. She claimed £100 for the house and '£43 in paper money and gold' which her prospective son-in-law had entrusted to her against his wedding on 19 June. There was also '£12 in property' in the same house!

A property manager complained that he had been prevented by the Military Authorities from collecting rents from tenants whose homes on Ella's Avenue, Waller Street, had been wrecked. It's an ill wind that blows nobody any good! Very few of the private claims relate to buildings, suggesting that most of the dispossessed were in rented property.

No doubt the prolonged stress caused some loss of efficiency and absenteeism from work due to loss of sleep, and this was not only in the towns. The logbooks of some rural schools on the Holderness Plain record pupils falling asleep or staying at home after nights disrupted by incoming or outgoing raiders. In Hull it was agreed that if the alarm sounded after dark the schools would close next day. For the younger citizens, a night sleeping in a ditch was a small price for such a bonus.

Another educational handicap was the requisitioning of schools by Home Defence troops, imposing 'time sharing' by the remaining establishments. Pupils would attend for half of each day - the morning one week and the afternoon the next. It is not supposed that this depressed them unduly.

The diversion of thousands of troops for anti-Zeppelin batteries and aerodromes was a definite gain for Germany from the bombing campaign; but it was a temporary advantage because the experience of coping with and combating the attacks was invaluable in preparing the defence system and civil organisation which enabled Britain to survive the infinitely heavier air raids of World War II.

The main significance of the Zeppelin bombing offensive for this story is that several examples of this feared and admired weapon fell into the hands of British airship designers.

III

The Submarine Crisis

When the light cruiser *HMS Pathfinder* was sunk by a torpedo from *U21* early in September 1914, it was not what the Royal Navy had been expecting at all. The Imperial German Navy had modern battleships and was expected to be a worthy opponent in open battle, which was considered to be inevitable at some time. The Royal Navy's superior numbers would not be of great advantage in such a conflict because many units were deployed on patrol duties and on various distant seas. The Imperial Navy's hope lay in enticing the British Grand Fleet from Scapa Flow to a suitable location for a short and decisive battle. Apart from the commerce raiders which were already roving at the outbreak of war, the German capital ships were a home-based strike force, with crews largely billeted on shore at Kiel and other Baltic ports until required for a sortie. By contrast the Royal Navy had to have units constantly at sea, blockading the enemy's supply routes and watching for the anticipated excursions of the Imperial Navy. The *Pathfinder* was on such a duty when she gave the first hint that the style of naval war was about to change.

The German High Command was well aware of the danger of being strangled by blockade before the Imperial Navy could sink the British Grand Fleet, and for several years had been developing a new naval weapon - the *Unterseeboot* or *U-boat*. The British had also toyed with the idea and had a few submarines of their own, but the Admiralty could not accept that such an underhand weapon would be used by a 'civilised' enemy. At the worst, it would be deployed against units of the fleet which could theoretically be protected by screens of destroyers and patrol boats armed with a few of the new depth charges then being developed. As for attacks on merchant shipping, the Prize Rules would apply, as they were part of international law. These rules (written for the regulation of commerce-raiding) specified that a ship could be stopped and searched, and if carrying goods for the enemy it could be taken as a prize; or sunk if no prize crew was available to take possession. In any case, neither passengers nor crew must be put at risk. No, submarine warfare was just too sneaky to contemplate!

It was the same sort of thinking which had convinced the Admiralty that aerial reconnaissance need not be taken seriously in naval warfare, as few pre-1914 aeroplanes could have lifted the heavy radio equipment of the day, and besides, the frail flying machines were at the mercy of the weather and therefore unreliable as scouts. It had not occurred to them that *airships* could carry wireless apparatus.

This is not the place to recount the squabbling of the pre-war years between the reformers - notably Admiral 'Jacky' Fisher - and the diehards of the traditional Navy, but the absence of a modern Naval Staff which was willing to study and anticipate new weapons gave the enemy some welcome opportunities for innovation.

Hard on the heels of the *Pathfinder* sinking, a major lesson was delivered on 22 September 1914, just seven weeks into the war, when the old cruisers *Aboukir, Hogue* and *Cressy* were torpedoed off the Dutch coast by one small coastal U-boat, with the loss of 1,450 lives. Following the rapid sinking of the *Aboukir*, her consorts had rushed to help and naively stopped to lower their boats, thus giving the submarine captain a hat trick and boosting the reputation of the new weapon back in Germany.

However, as if to reassure the British 'gentlemen', when the first merchant ship, the *SS Glitra* of 866 tons, was sunk on 20 October by U-17, it was strictly in accordance with the Prize Rules. A shot was fired across her bows, her nationality was confirmed by a boarding party, and the crew allowed to launch their boats before the *Glitra's* seacocks were opened.

But there was another shock on 27 October 1914 when the modern Dreadnought, *HMS Audacious*, was sunk by a *mine* off the north coast of Ireland, the sinking being witnessed by passengers on the White Star liner *Olympic*. In the futile hope of keeping it quiet the *Olympic* was taken to Lough Swilly, where the passengers' discretion was requested. As there were a number of neutrals on board, including Americans who had photographed the sinking, the news broke first in the foreign press, starting rumours of an even greater cover-up by the British censor.

By now both sides were busy laying mines around their coasts, not only as defence against invasion or naval attack, but increasingly as a means of blockade of each other's supply routes. On the British side this was supplemented by surface patrols (including older warships, converted ocean liners and trawlers) and on the German side by a rapid expansion of submarine warfare and commerce raiding by roving surface ships. The Germans, who had the lead in mine technology, also developed mine-laying submarines. Early successes by the commerce raiders were eventually reduced by conventional naval hounding, but the twin threats of mine and submarine were not so easily met. Shipping losses rapidly increased until it looked as if Britain, not Germany, would lose the blockade contest. U-boats would attack with torpedoes or more boldly by gunfire on the surface, easily evading the widely scattered naval escorts. There was a reluctance at first to concentrate ships into convoys and lone ships were easy targets. *Q-ships* - armed decoys - had some initial success but mainly in making U-boat captains less inclined to surface where they might face a trap. Net and mine barriers were laid across U-boat routes and harbour mouths and naval patrols were increased in known submarine hunting grounds. Hasty experiments with floatplanes and shipborne aircraft were ultimately to lead to aircraft tenders and carriers and to the development of large flying boats, but when in 1915 the threat of the U-boat blockade was first recognised, it was to the airshipmen that the Admiralty turned in desperation.

Admiral Jacky Fisher, recalled from retirement to be the First Sea Lord in October 1914, sent for the airshipmen on 28 February 1915. He asked them to produce, in the shortest possible time, a scouting craft capable of finding submarines. Fortunately they had anticipated the need and were able to suggest that a small and easily constructed non-rigid airship would be suitable. Fisher told them to have the prototype ready in three weeks. The men who developed the idea had an interesting mix of experience and talent. Wing Commander Usborne, RN, was an ex-submariner and torpedo expert who had also been on the HMA No.1 *Mayfly* project at Barrow. His young colleague Flight Lieutenant Hicks was a skilful airship pilot. Wing Commander Cave-Brown-Cave, in charge of non-rigid airship design at Kingsnorth, was a formally trained Royal Naval engineer with long design experience in battleships and submarines who had transferred to airship design and also qualified as an airship pilot. In consultation with Mr F. M. Greene, Chief Engineer of the Royal Aircraft Factory at Farnborough, they devised a prototype utilising existing parts - a spare envelope of the Army airship *Eta* and a wingless BE2c aeroplane fuselage and engine. Thus the prototype *Submarine Scout* was cobbled together, with the addition of simple control surfaces on the envelope and a pipe set in the slipstream to inflate the air ballonets. The bow was stiffened by cane battens to preserve the shape when at speed. A fourteen gallon water tank behind the pilot provided 140 lbs of ballast and racks for small bombs were fixed to the undercarriage. Petrol was carried in three tanks, but had to be hand-pumped from the two lower ones to the small gravity tank above the engine. A Lewis gun on a pillar mount completed the armament. The observer-engineer-gunner-W/T operator sat in the front seat surrounded by the bulkier components of the crude wireless apparatus. Later models had a third, rather exposed seat behind the pilot for an engineer, who would have to climb along the landing skids to tend the temperamental engine and to restart it by swinging the propeller with one hand.

Initial trials were completed by the end of March and modifications by 11 April. On 7 May SS.1 set off for operational service at Capel, near Dover, but fouled some telegraph wires in the dusk and burned out. By good fortune the crew of two escaped, and Flight Lieutenant Booth lived to become one of the most illustrious British airshipmen. This accident did not halt the *Submarine Scout* programme, as the forceful Jacky Fisher had already been convinced and had ordered forty, eighteen of which were in service by the end of 1915.

A second experimental envelope made of doped aeroplane fabric had proved to be leaky, and it was decided to use rubberised fabric, the envelope for SS.3 being assigned to Short Brothers at Cardington. This being successful, further builders were needed, and several manufacturers of rainwear found a new and lucrative outlet for their materials and talents, working in converted premises such as ballrooms and halls. The patterns were supplied as aluminium templates with holes drilled to mark the corners of the panels, and each template could hold the keys to a number of panel shapes, enabling the fabric to be quickly marked out by pencil dots. Even the templates could be mass-produced by drilling through a stack of sheets.

Much of the work was done by women - of great significance as the casualties mounted on both land and sea. From early 1916 it was the policy to recruit women for airship building, including the massive rigids, and the Vickers factory ultimately employed 60% female airship workers.

As experience was gained with the SS ships other aeroplane fuselages were utilised, including Maurice Farman and Armstrong-Whitworth types. The Farman version had the advantage of a 'pusher' engine which gave the crew some relief from the slipstream. Further experience led to the designing of special control cars, such as the floating car for the SS-Zero type airship and the two engined version for the SS-Twin. Many of the improvements were thought up and applied by the aircrews and ground staff on the operational stations, often ignoring orders which forbade modifications.

The origin of the nickname 'blimp' is not certain. One version is that the original SS ships with BE2 cars were known as *B-type limps* - hence *B-limp*. It is also suggested that *blimp* is an onomatopoeic word

Fig. 5 A victim of the U-Boat war.

Fig. 6 A Submarine Scout blimp. The control car is a BE2c aeroplane fuselage. In the background, a Coastal Class airship. (Photo: Mrs V. Maclean)

Fig. 7 Blimps signalled U-boat or mine sightings to surface craft by Aldis lamp
or by dropping a flare or smoke marker.

Fig. 8 The car of a Zero type Submarine Scout, armed with bombs,
flares and Lewis gun. The boat-shaped hull could alight on the sea.

for the sound made when the inflated envelope was slapped as a rough test of pressure.

Even before the Submarine Scouts had proved themselves, the development of larger *pressure* airships with increased endurance and lifting power was under way. The first expedient was to utilise the Astra-Torres trilobe envelope (built originally as HMA No.8) to create the *Coastal Class*, with a car made from two Avro fuselages joined back to back and suspended by means of internal curtains in the envelope, which supported wires passing through glands in the fabric. This allowed the crew to be increased to four or five, with a steering cox'n or second pilot (doubling as observer) to relieve the captain. At least one member would be trained to operate the car-mounted Lewis gun, and in later ships a second gun position was provided on top of the envelope, accessible by a rope ladder in a canvas tube. The first of these unlovely but sturdy ships, C.1, was tested on 31 May 1915 and thirty were ultimately built.

A later refinement, the *C-Star (C*)* had a larger streamlined envelope and increased duration of officially 15 hours. C*4 (Captain F. Cleary) logged 34 hours and 30 minutes on patrol from Howden in May 1918, showing what could be achieved by an experienced crew.

As these little craft were being assembled there was a parallel urgent programme of recruitment and training of crews, initially by volunteers from the Royal Navy. These would include both experienced airminded officers and youngsters looking for excitement. Inevitably there would be some who were encouraged by their superiors to make the change, through being temperamentally unsuited to formal naval discipline. The engineers, observers and wireless operators were drafted as volunteers from the lower deck, until a training programme could be set up for recruits enrolling directly into the Royal Naval Air Service for both aeroplanes and airships. The aspiring airship captains would first have to qualify as balloon pilots, flying in hydrogen balloons from Hurlingham polo ground, a satellite of Wormwood Scrubs Airship Station. This free-ballooning experience was essential to a pilot who might frequently have to land a blimp after engine failure, when it would not only be at the mercy of wind and relying solely on *static* lift, but would most likely be distinctly 'non-rigid' by losing the air pressure in the ballonets. In any case a thorough knowledge of *aerostatics* (the science of lighter-than-air flight) was necessary to fly what was little more than a balloon with a low-powered engine, depending for its endurance on conserving fuel by minimum use of dynamic lift.

Having qualified by way of a solo cross-country balloon flight, the budding airshipman would be given a ride in a powered *non-rigid*, before being posted on a series of courses - in navigation, engines, gunnery, meteorology, rigging and signalling; as well as drill and administration. Finally, flying instruction would be given, but not necessarily at the official training stations such as Kingsnorth or Cranwell. If the demand was urgent, the instruction might be completed at an operational station under the guidance of an experienced pilot.

While the major *rigid* airship bases were still unfinished the blimps got on with the job, and very soon there was a chain of stations for anti-submarine patrols round the coasts of Great Britain and Ireland, with a number of mooring-out stations where shelter could be found in woods or quarries. For the first time since the start of the U-boat campaign the rate of sinkings dropped dramatically. It was also found that mines were visible from the air in calm seas, enabling ships to be diverted and minesweepers called up. In practice the *Submarine Scout* and its larger consorts which were rapidly developed (the *Coastals* and the *North Sea Class*) could do little damage to a submerged U-boat, but they could frighten it into submerging and thus both blind it and slow it down, enabling the escorted ships to escape; or they could mark its position with a flame-float and summon surface ships by Aldis lamp for a conventional depth-charge attack.

The slow speed, steadiness and endurance of the *non-rigid* airship offered advantages over the aeroplanes of the day, although some inshore cover was given by landplanes and floatplanes until flying boats later took over the longer patrols, particularly in areas subject to interference from German fighter floatplanes.

The ultimate in development of *pressure* airships was the *North Sea Class*, with an extended range, enclosed accommodation and sleeping provision for a spare crew. They had a performance better than some of the rigids. Designed for 21 hours endurance, NS.11 once remained airborne for over 100 hours to establish a record.

As both *Coastal* and *NS* types could not easily be moored out and required sizeable permanent sheds, they normally operated from the larger airship stations, including those which they shared with the *rigids*.

Later, when the first big *rigids* became operational, they were found to be of limited use against submarines because of the trouble of getting them into the air. However, they carried a respectable bomb load, and R.29 was credited with helping to sink UB-115 off Newbiggin Point in September 1918, for which her captain, Major G. M. Thomas, received the DFC. At that time he was operating from East Fortune but we shall meet him again in Yorkshire. R.29, built by Armstrong-Whitworth at Barlow, near Selby, and modelled on the earlier military Zeppelins, was one of the more robust and useful of the British rigid airships.

The anti-submarine blimp was to become a familiar sight round the coasts of the British Isles between 1916 and 1919, as the chain of stations grew and most coastal and cross-channel traffic was escorted while weather permitted. As the cover was extended it was necessary to provide temporary facilities at remote sites as far apart as the Scillies and Orkneys and at several locations in Ireland and the Isle of Man. In some places a temporary shed was provided, but *mooring-out stations* might consist only of a clearing cut in a wood with tented accommodation for the personnel. Howden had two such satellites - at Lowthorpe near Bridlington and Kirkleathham near Redcar. Screw pickets or buried concrete blocks would anchor the SS ships with the assistance of sandbags attached to the handling guys. Occasionally a blimp would escape, or would snag on its protective trees. As a regular operator from Lowthorpe, George Meager experienced most of the hazards of mooring-out, including flying into a tree near the landing ground. The resulting punctures were beyond local repair, and SS-Z.32 was rolled up and dispatched to the parent station by lorry. Escaping a reprimand by the benevolence of the First Officer of RNAS Howden (Lieutenant Commander Blatherwick) he may have later reflected that this accident could have been fatal in an aeroplane. He was again 'on the carpet' when SS-Z.54 was torn when emerging from the clearing in the wood, but convinced the Court of Inquiry that the exit needed widening. A dedicated and skilful airshipman, Captain Meager, AFC, was later to become First Officer of R.100.

The cars of the SS-Zero ships were custom-built to give better comfort and reliability, including safer access to the engine, than in the early Submarine Scouts. Although later BE2c type control cars had a third cockpit added for the engineer, this was standard - and better protected from weather - in the SS-Z car, which was designed to float so that the blimp could be landed on water to retrieve objects or liaise with surface craft. Such liaison might include the purchase or barter of fish from boats for the Officers' Mess! A practice bomb could also bring stunned fish to the surface for collection but was more profitable if it could be dropped within sight of a small boat manned by RNAS personnel, as local fishermen were soon wise to this bonus from practice bombing.

It was later the proud boast of the RNAS airshipmen that no ship or convoy which they escorted had suffered loss, and while this may be true they could not be everywhere at once, and twice during the Great War the submarines nearly won. It was the first crisis in early 1915 which had brought the Submarine Scout into existence. Between January and May of that year 232,000 tons of *merchant* shipping had been sunk, but it was the sinking of the liner *Lusitania* on 7 May with the loss of 1,257 passengers which caught the headlines. The international outcry (especially in America) caused the German High Command to temporarily prohibit the unrestricted sinking of passenger ships except under the Prize Rules. But by August the relentless campaign was on again, with 165,000 tons of merchant shipping lost to the U-boats and a further 20,800 tons to mines and other causes. However, when U-24 sank the British liner *Arabic* off Ireland there were three more American dead, and the resulting furore so alarmed the German High Command that they switched many of their submarines to the Mediterranean and Aegean where ships were abundant and escorts (and Americans) were scarce. This glut of targets was largely due to the Dardanelles (Gallipoli) campaign and the Salonika (Macedonian) operations of 1915 and 1916. The vast numbers of British, French and Dominion troops were supported by a huge armada of merchant and naval ships, inadequately protected by either sea or air patrols. A U-boat could disport itself like a fox among chickens, choosing fat targets at anchor or on known supply routes. Apart from the material losses and the considerable death toll on the crowded transports - the loss of the troopship *Royal Edward* with 336 casualties being the worst single incident - the U-boat threat was bad for morale, already suffering from the terrible losses in the Gallipoli Peninsula and from the dysentery which caused even more deaths than the Turks. The author's grandfather died of dysentery at Mudros, and his ship, *HMS Redbreast*, was later sunk with all hands.

As a rather feeble gesture, in spite of strong campaigning by Rear Admiral Sueter (one of the earliest airship enthusiasts at the Admiralty), an Airship Expeditionary Force was hastily formed, under Flight Commander E. H. Sparling, and a few of the new Submarine Scouts were packed off on *HMS Mooltan* to the Eastern Mediterranean, escorted through the Bay of Biscay by destroyers and blimps. At Imbros Island the airship equipment had to be rescued from the surf after a barge capsized, but by 13 September 1915 a portable shed had been erected and SS.7 made its first flight. Following 'trouble with the shed', (probably because it was suspected of attracting the frequent bombings of Imbros by German aircraft) the base was moved to Mudros, where SS.19 and SS.3 were also inflated, flown by Sub Lieutenants T. P. York-Moore and J. E. M. Pritchard. SS.17 and SS.41 were also dispatched, but do not appear to have been inflated at Mudros, and were most likely sent direct to Kassandra in Northern Greece to support the Salonika operations. Unspectacular though their efforts may have been in comparison with the activity of Commander Samson's aeroplanes of the seaplane carrier *Ark Royal*, they undoubtedly proved their worth in spotting mines and expended torpedoes, as well as deterring an unknown number of U-boat attacks, where the clear Mediterranean and Aegean waters were ideal for airship reconnaissance.

While the summer flying weather of 1916 may have been kinder than in British coastal waters, the airship personnel shared the same miserable rations, primitive conditions and the dysentery and sandfly fever which plagued the troops. In November 1916 J. E. M. Pritchard was invalided home to recuperate from dysentery, followed by a posting to RN Airship Station Polegate as Senior Flying Officer. He had not joined the RNAS until 24 May 1915, and had only qualified as Airship Pilot in August of that year, but with practical operational experience he was soon instructing as well as doing routine patrols. We shall meet him again later.

* * *

Fortunately for Britain, grievous though the shipping losses had been in the Mediterranean, the absence of the U-boats from home waters had given temporary and welcome relief from the loss of vital supplies coming from America and the Empire. Until February 1916 the Royal Navy had a chance to improve its defensive tactics, while the shipyards could gear themselves up to replace the lost tonnage. This was relief at a critical time, although there were other crises still to come, the closest call being during April 1917 when 881,000 tons of merchant shipping was sunk, mostly by submarines. This was not even equalled during the worst month of the 'Battle of the Atlantic' in World War II. These record losses reduced the United Kingdom's reserves of food and other essentials to an estimated six weeks, and if they had continued like this Britain would probably have sought peace terms. With the Americans about to join the Allies, the Germans had finally decided on all-out *unrestricted* submarine warfare against *all* shipping trading with Britain. Fortunately a co-ordinated plan of nets, mines, patrols and air cover narrowly saved the situation. But it was the belated introduction of the convoy system which made the air cover really effective for the first time.

* * *

It is difficult to give a definite figure for the number of airship stations which were involved in the anti-submarine war, as some stations had dual functions such as training or testing. There were the temporary mooring-out facilities and places where portable sheds were used. There were also some which were not completed in time for active use between 1915 and 1918. An approximate figure of forty gives some idea of the scale of provision, but it is surprising that not many more than 200 blimps were built, with 103 in commission at the Armistice in November 1918. These figures indicate the very high efficiency of the service, which carried out its duties with great success in spite of being spread so thinly. It says much for the endurance and dedication of the aircrews and the people who did the difficult and often dangerous servicing and handling on the ground. Fire was a constant danger, as petrol and hydrogen were frequently topped up in the sheds, and the resulting fumes could be easily ignited by sparks from the primitive wireless equipment or engines under test. Such an accident ignited an SS-Zero ship in the No.1 Shed at Howden in August 1918, taking with it two other SS-Z's and the rigid R.27. Ten airships were burned in their sheds during the war and a further two in the air. Hydrogen is a highly inflammable gas, as anyone who has seen the often screened newsreel of the *Hindenberg* disaster will know. When pure it is relatively safe, but mixed with air it is potentially explosive. The mixing could happen externally because of a leak, or internally by contamination by air seeping from the ballonets. The purity (i.e. ratio of hydrogen to air) had to be carefully watched for this reason, apart from the loss of buoyancy of impure gas. Smoking near an airship was strictly taboo, as were studded boots when working aloft in a steel-framed airship shed.

The signing of the Armistice on 11 November 1918 did not immediately end the role of the Royal Naval airships, as there was the immense task of detecting and recovering the minefields. The formation of the Royal Air Force (by the amalgamation of the RNAS and the RFC on 1 April 1918) created certain anomalies, and for some time the airships were still owned by the Admiralty but crewed by nominal RAF personnel - probably still wearing RNAS uniform.

Their task had been unglamorous and tiresome, but the dramatic reduction in sinkings following the introduction of the little airships was a source of great pride to the service.

By comparison with the massive toll of men in the land and sea battles the casualty rate was not high, but it was a small and integrated service and the losses were felt keenly.

Only two airships (C.17 and C.27) are known to have been lost by enemy action, but forced landings at sea were frequent and often fatal.

It is ironic that in World War II the U-boat once again caught Britain unprepared and came close to winning the Battle of the Atlantic. By this time, with greater range and speed of both aircraft and submarines, it was not possible to give much cover by small airships. Only off the eastern seaboard of America, in the Caribbean and briefly in the Straits of Gibraltar did the blimp again contribute to the defeat of the U-boat campaign.

IV

Howden

Howden is an ancient market town near the confluence of the great rivers which drain Yorkshire and merge into the Humber Estuary. The Prince Bishops of Durham, advisers to the King, had a summer palace here and also used it as a staging post on the journey to London. King John brought his court here in 1191 and in 1206 granted the town a charter to hold markets and fairs. King Edward II came on a pilgrimage to the tomb of St. John of Howden and Henry V came to pardon the son of Glendower for some misdeed of his father! Over the centuries the Howden Horse Fair became the precursor of an international motor show, supplying the cavalry of European armies and domestic, agricultural and industrial horsepower well into the 19th Century. Stabling and feeding thousands of horses and accommodating buyers and sellers were nice little earners to supplement the normal commerce of a busy market town. With the coming of the canals and railway much of the business shifted to the newly accessible industrial Doncaster, but it was the electric tramcar and the internal combustion engine which hastened the end of the great horse fairs.

By 1914 much of Howden's glory had faded into history and the two railways which served the town were only passing to more important destinations. The nearby upstart port of Goole was another rival, thriving at the conjunction of navigable waterways which reached inland to the coal and iron towns of Yorkshire and where cargoes to and from the Continent could be transhipped.

The surrounding flatland is predominantly agricultural but subject to periodic flooding and to frequent mists or merciless winds in winter. Apart from the rivers and canals the landscape might best be described as featureless, but there is even now no denying the charm and cosiness of the old town, still showing many traces of its former functions - not least a goodly selection of inns, a fine minster church and the restored Bishop's Manor.

In August 1915 the Admiralty dispatched Royal Naval Lieutenants Flower and Burke to the Humber area to select a site for a major airship base, suitably placed to cover the important East Coast ports; one of a number of stations required for the new giant dirigibles which were on order for the Royal Naval Air Service. They selected a site three miles north of Howden, between the diverging roads to Bubwith and Spaldington. By 27 September the Admiralty had purchased one thousand acres of farmland and work started at once to provide access by rail and road. Howden was once more in the news and in the money as contractors and naval personnel moved in, many lodging in the town or neighbouring farms and villages. Pending the completion of permanent sheds, a portable Bessoneaux hanger - canvas on a wooden framework - was dispatched from RNAS Walney Island in March 1916, followed by the Commanding Officer designate of RNAS Howden, Wing Commander F. L. M. Boothby. As an additional contribution Walney Island sent out four aeroplanes - three Bristol Boxkites and a Curtiss JN3 - to be used for familiarisation flights by the airship pilots who were awaiting delivery of their own craft. As these aircraft were already somewhat dated, the transfer was most likely in the nature of 'clearing the attic' at Walney Island. However it was sensible at that early stage of aviation to have pilots qualified to fly both airships and aeroplanes and many of the hastily recruited young aviators were given this opportunity, subject to the intermittent serviceability of the aircraft.

Meanwhile the Admiralty constructors were busy laying out facilities appropriate to a small town, including water, sewage, roads, electric light, telephones, railway sidings and an essential and comprehensive system of drains. In addition to barrack huts and officers' quarters there were a post office, chapel, YMCA and a pigeon loft. The comfortable and substantial Brindcommon Farm, temporarily occupied by the Royal Navy, was demolished to clear the approach to the landing field.

Beyond the accommodation and office blocks, but still to the left of the long approach road, was the technical area, dominated by the huge hydrogen gas works. Here also were the electric power house, the workshops, stores and fuel dumps.

To the right of the approach road and strictly parallel to it, Navy style, were the three airship sheds - initially the standard pattern of one *Rigid* Shed flanked by two smaller sheds of the *Coastal* pattern which also served as windbreaks for the emerging rigids. Separate wind screens also extended forward from the Coastal Sheds and another shielded the rear approach to the Rigid Shed. Large concrete ducts carried the hydrogen and water mains to these buildings.

Fig. 9 The technical site of Howden airship station. (Photo: Public Record Office)

Fig. 10 Old and new technology side by side. (Photo: Public Record Office)

Fig. 11 Coastal Class C4 operated from Howden with Consorts C.11, C.19 and C.21.
They were known locally as 'The Howden Pigs'.

Fig. 12 No.2 (Double Rigid) shed at Howden Airship Station

Essential to any airship base was a copious supply of water, which not only served the domestic needs of the site, but also supplied the tons of ballast required by the large rigids and more modest demands of the blimps. Conversely, water was a raw material of hydrogen manufactured by the steam-over-coke process which was employed at Howden and thus indirectly provided the lift as well as the ballast. It took three wells, a powerful pumping station and two water towers to concentrate a ready supply of this basic commodity.

To serve the needs of men and machines a branch railway line was built from Howden North Station, running alongside the Bubwith road before crossing the airfield diagonally. Its various sidings terminated at coal and coke drops - complete with weighbridge for fair measure - and at the fuel dump, domestic and technical stores. Spurs even entered the airship sheds. Later, when No.2 Double Rigid Shed was added, it too was served by rail. For obvious reasons, steam locomotives were barred from sheds which housed inflated airships, and a horse would complete the haul. Straddling the track where it crossed the approach road, a large double gantry enabled heavy loads to be transferred from rail to road transport. On occasions a neatly rolled blimp envelope and its car would arrive by train for inflation on site, as portability was one of the incidental virtues of a *pressure* airship. Among its vices was the vulnerability of the fabric to puncturing, in which case the deflated envelope and impotent control car would be returned to base by lorry or rail, while the unfortunate pilot would concoct what he hoped would be an acceptable written explanation.

It is interesting to surmise whether the RAF euphemism 'tearing off a strip' - meaning a verbal reprimand - derived metaphorically from doing to an airman what he had done to the fabric of an airship or aeroplane.

As the work progressed at Howden an Admiralty photographer was dispatched to record the growth and the completed buildings, from the massive rigid sheds to the humble pigeon loft. Looking at these frozen images one is struck by the contrast of the technologies involved. The huge steel and concrete structures - on the scale of the Pyramids - are being pieced together by human labour aided by steam and horse power. Foundations are dug by men with picks and shovels. Rail tracks not only bring the materials but also bear the massive scaffolding which shuffles forward as the building grows. Horses and carts supplement the motor lorries and steam traction engines on site. All is controlled from the site supervisor's wooden hut with its coke stove and attendant bicycle. The finished structures, containing as much steel as a battleship and whose doors each weigh 150 tons, will house 700 feet giants which will float on air.

On their journeys, the giants will each carry two carrier pigeons as backup for their temperamental wireless transmitters. The pigeons also have the edge in navigational skill - at least on home runs - but that is jumping ahead of our story.

Site works were still in progress when Commander E. A. D. Masterman's Rigid Airship Trial flight was established at Howden Airship Station in May 1916, in anticipation of the delivery of HMA No.9, still under construction at the Vickers factory at Walney Island, Barrow-in-Furness. In fact No.9 did not fly until 27 November 1916, and as she was unable to lift her contract weight - a mere 3.1 tons - she had to be considerably modified and did not reach Howden until May 1917. She had also been delayed by demarcation strikes, and by the Irish Easter Rising of 1916 which interrupted supplies of flax for the gasbag netting. Meanwhile the trial crew spent much time at Barrow, co-operating with the designer H. B. Pratt and his young assistant B. N. Wallis.

To explain the numbering of British airships it is necessary to mention the capricious nature of both design and policy dating from the earliest experiments with lighter-than-air flight. Before 1914 the few Army airships, which had been developed experimentally or bought in from designers at home and abroad, were designated by their makers' names (e.g. *Astra-Torres, Willows*) or Greek letters with sometimes a series number added.

When the Naval Wing of the RFC (soon to be known as the Royal Naval Air Service) took over the Army airships in January 1914 the methodical Navy allocated numbers and the prefix *His Majesty's Airship* to all its charges. HMA No.1 having previously broken its back in 1911 before flying, HMA No.9 was only the Navy's second *rigid* airship, and before it was even completed there were other smaller *limp* airships with higher numbers, including the ex-army ships *Gamma II* (HMA No.18) and *Eta I* (HMA No.20). Also, the numbering of designs on the drawing board (often never completed) and leaving numbers for repeat orders meant that there were gaps in the sequence. In fact the next *rigids* to actually fly after No.9 were Nos. 23, 24 and 25. From No.26 onwards all *rigids* had the 'R' prefix and *non-rigids* had a class letter and serial number, e.g. SS.3 (Submarine Scout No.3) or C.11 (Coastal No.11).

It was this latter ship which opened Howden for business on 26 June 1916, arriving by air from Kingsnorth, the constructional station on the Medway. However it was C.4, received by rail and assembled on site, which made the first *outward* flight on 3 July, piloted by Sub-Lieutenant Ralph Booth, who as Captain of R.100 in 1929 was to have the unique distinction of making the first and last flights from Howden. On this first occasion he followed the Humber Estuary to Spurn Point, hugged the coast to Flamborough and returned overland. Not to be outdone, C.11 showed the flag over Selby and York in the afternoon.

Next to arrive were C.19 and C.21, giving the station a workable but unglamorous quartet, soon to be known locally as 'The Howden Pigs'. As if to emphasise their plainness, the elegant *Parseval* P.4 was received by rail for assembly - the envelope in July and the car in August. This German-designed ship was one of four built or modified by Vickers at Barrow under a prewar licensing agreement negotiated by Captain Murray F. Sueter (see chapter 5). The Coastals were immediately busy on shipping patrols, covering the essential traffic which hugged the East Coast and was particularly vulnerable when converging towards the estuarine ports of the Humber, Tees and the Wash, and also when edging round Flamborough Head. At the limits of their area they sometimes sighted their complementary patrols operating from Norfolk and Scotland. The more glamorous *Parseval*, although a non-rigid ship, was sophisticated enough to train the Trials Flight as they waited for No.9. This small, elite group of experienced airship personnel had been hand-picked for the job, as it was inexperience which was deemed to have wrecked No.1. Commodore (later Wing Captain) Masterman was determined that No.9 would not suffer in the same way. Described as 'one of the few thinkers in the *rigid* programme', Masterman had commanded the Naval Airship Wing at Farnborough during the early experimental days. He was a close friend of Major Edward Maitland who had been Commanding Officer of the Air Battalion of the Royal Engineers at Farnborough and first Commanding Officer of the No.1 Squadron Royal Flying Corps when it was formed in 1912. These two were to be associated with all the early rigid airships and particularly with Howden Airship Station. It is necessary and fair to add that other 'thinkers' were to appear later in the rigid airship programme but they were bedevilled by the decisions (and vacillations) of less able but more powerful men.

To avoid confusion and the possible irritation of the reader, it seems wise to explain also the inconsistent ranks held by individuals as the story progresses. The Royal Flying Corps had many seconded officers who retained their Army-style titles and often continued to wear their regimental uniforms. Functional titles such as Flight Commander did not necessarily reflect the substantive rank, which might be Captain, for example. NCOs and below might have a trade-related designation, such as Air Mechanic or Flight Sergeant.

In the Royal Naval Air Service the standard naval ranks were sometimes embellished by the prefix 'Wing' or 'Flight'. When in 1918 the two services merged as the Royal Air Force there was a period of adjustment during which existing titles were retained until the next promotion, when there was a regrading into a new RAF rank. In addition there were transfers between services, which, for example, transformed Masterman from Wing Captain, RN, to a Brigadier General in the Army. As far as possible, I will try to use ranks contemporary with each stage of the story.

For the moment, let us return to Howden in 1916, an airship station manned by the RNAS and a number of civilian employees. There were also members of the Air Service Constructional Corps. The Women's Services had yet to appear, but would come to play a significant part in the airship story.

As for the sheds, they were engineering marvels in their own right, the largest being on the scale of cathedrals but requiring a clear span without internal supports and being capable of suspending a deflated airship weighing up to 150 tons. Whereas a cathedral might take centuries to complete, the housing for the new aerial fleet had to be completed in months, made more urgent by the U-boat crisis in 1915. By the time of the Armistice in 1918 over sixty sheds had been built in the United Kingdom (which included all of Ireland at that time), and others were under construction or planned both at home and in the Mediterranean.

Initially Howden had only the standard trio of one *Rigid* and two *Coastal* sheds but was to have the largest shed in the world by 1919. The No.2 *Double Rigid Shed* measured 750 feet internally (228.6m) with two 150 feet (45.7m) bays and had a *clearance* height of 130 feet (39.6m) at the doors. If Nelson's column had been erected inside, the Admiral would have poked through the 170 feet apex of the roof from the knees upwards. In addition to the berthing space, the *Rigid* sheds each had two 35 feet (10.7m) annexes along their flanks to serve as work and storage spaces.

The nearby Howden Minister - a very large church - could have been accommodated six times inside. Next time you take a walk, try pacing out the 250 yard length of the shed; or superimpose its outline to scale on your local street plan.

By comparison the *Coastal* sheds measured a mere 324 feet (98.7m) x 110 feet (33.5m) x 80 feet (24.3m), about half the area of a football pitch.

These buildings were innovative, perhaps owing more to the art of the bridge builder or shipwright than the architect, with massive steel arches clad in corrugated sheeting. Staircases and walkways threaded through the steel web, giving access to the tops of berthed airships for maintenance or for attaching suspension slings. Needless to say, no heating of this vast space was possible - even if it had been permissible in the presence of hydrogen - bearing in mind that the ubiquitous coke stove was the serviceman's main source of warmth and could be brought to red heat by a determined stoker. Whilst later generations of aircraft workers will remember the discomfort of the winter maintenance, the airshipman had the hazard of cold hands on frosted girders, with a fall of a hundred-plus feet if he lost his grip. There was the added danger of losing consciousness when repairing a hydrogen leak and plunging through the gasbag to the wires and girders below. One such accident had an ultimately happy outcome for Chief Petty Officer George Cook of the Trial Crew. While searching for leaks he was overcome by hydrogen and fell through the ship, sustaining serious injuries. Unfit for flying, he became involved in mooring experiments and as Flying Officer Cook, RAF, he became Mooring Tower Officer at Pulham and later at Cardington. But even with the smaller blimps it was not unknown for a rigger, creeping carefully over the top to inspect a valve, to be dropped into the envelope through the sudden splitting of ageing fabric. This would entail some rapid surgery with a sheath knife by a colleague, and a breath-holding dash to extract the victim.

At the same time that Howden Airship Station was giving a new profile to the Yorkshire flatlands, other major stations were rising at Cranwell, Pulham in Norfolk, East Fortune near Edinburgh and Longside near Aberdeen. There were also rigid airship *constructional* stations in hand at Barlow, near Selby (Armstrong-Whitworth), Inchinnan on the Clyde (Beardmore) and Cardington (Short Brothers). These were in addition to the existing building facilities of Vickers at Barrow, and the main non-rigid factory at Kingsnorth. One rigid shed was erected at Cramlington in Northumberland, but too late to be of service in the war. Others proposed for Cork, Lough Neagh and Flookborough, Lancashire, were never completed.

The numerous smaller operational stations may have been less sophisticated than the permanent bases for rigid airships, but what they lacked in comfort was compensated by a freer atmosphere and lack of the 'big ship' mentality which some of the younger personnel found irksome. For example, Howden had two parade grounds and a 'quarterdeck', and as much shipboard routine as could be adapted to the running of an air station. In an attempt to maintain standards of discipline a number of regular Royal Naval non-flying personnel, including senior officers, were posted to the Royal Naval Air Service. This led to some quaint situations, as when a pilot had made a heavy landing he might have to face a Court of Inquiry or even a Court Martial for 'Hazarding his Ship'.

V

The Human Element

From the reminiscences, both written and oral, of former airship people and their friends, it is possible to have a fairly clear picture of their lives. Allowing for the mellowing of memories with time and the nostalgia factor it is clear that in spite of the anomalies, hardships and danger there was excellent morale and close kinship in the lighter-than-air community. The necessary mobility of ships and personnel meant that inter-station rivalries were not strong, as members were frequently moved between bases. Inevitably there were occasional clashes of interest or personality as would occur in any organisation, but such annoyances were endurable in the short term when weighed against the importance of the job. Perhaps understandably, there was a trace of 'class-consciousness' between those working on rigids and the aircrews and riggers on the blimps. The same snobbishness existed in the 'real' navy between the crews of the big ships and little ships, but it was diluted somewhat in the RNAS by the need to service any type of airship which presented itself. And of course it was the height of folly for a Lieutenant, RN, proud captain of an SS-Zero, to pull rank on the Chief Petty Officer of a handling party.

As always in war, there were wide discrepancies in age and comfort between those directing and those doing the work. At the Admiralty, now reluctantly accepting war in *three* dimensions both above and below sea-level, there were a few aviation specialists responsible for design, supply, finance, personnel and general management. As most were comparatively senior men, they had gained their experience and advancement in a more conventional navy, and they were sometimes reluctant to call in the new technology in time or in sufficient quantity. The entire history of British lighter-than-air flight reveals squabbling and vacillation at the Admiralty and later at the Air Ministry. The friction extended to

Fig. 13 An exclusively female handling party brings out a SS-Zero, 'weighed-off' with its crew on board for a patrol.

Fig. 14 A North Sea Class non-rigid airship prepares for flight. With a theoretical endurance of 21 hours they carried a crew of ten to allow for rest periods.

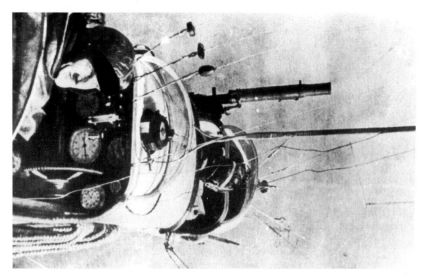

Fig. 15 The captain of a SS-Zero.
(Photo: Mrs V. Maclean)

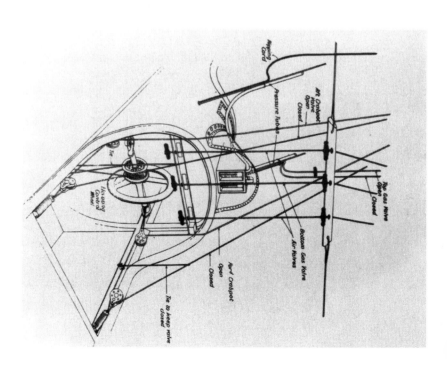

Fig. 16 The controls of the SS-Zero.

Vickers, traditional armourers of the Royal Navy and the first to be asked to build the British rigids. There were accusations of profiteering and deviousness on the one hand and parsimony and bad faith on the other. The new constructors - Armstrong-Whitworth, Beardmore and Short Brothers - were soon drawn into the arguments. Also, it was not helpful that the Director of Air Services and Superintendent of Airship Construction (holding the title of Fifth Sea Lord) had no control of *operations*. All *operational* control was in the hands of the Royal Navy, whose officers were not directly answerable to the Fifth Sea Lord. To the younger airminded men, this made it more difficult to apply their enthusiasm, experience and initiative against the wishes of their immediate superiors, who had no wish to antagonise their Lordships at the Admiralty by endorsing heretical new notions about the threat which aerial reconnaissance posed to naval forces.

The tribulations of Captain Murray F. Sueter (later Rear Admiral Sir Murray Sueter) are typical of this period of change. An early submariner, he was a member of the 'Fishpond' - the group of technically-minded young officers who surrounded Admiral 'Jacky' Fisher. He became interested in aviation and was appointed Inspecting Captain of Airships. After the *'Mayfly'* fiasco, he was placed on half-pay while the future of airships was debated, but brought back in charge of the Admiralty Air Department when the Royal Flying Corps was formed in May 1912. His suggestions for the use of *'Mayfly'* for mooring experiments and for the use of blimps with the blockading forces were never forwarded to the influential Committee of Imperial Defence.

With Colonel Mervyn O'Gorman, Superintendent of Farnborough Royal Aircraft Factory, he visited Germany in June 1912 to evaluate the *Parseval* non-rigid airship, which was purchased for the Royal Navy as HMA No.4 and modified at Barrow. Convinced that airships were a weapon of the future, he found himself opposed by First Lord of the Admiralty Winston Churchill, and all the leading admirals apart from Fisher and Jellicoe. He complained to a friend that it 'was impossible to get new ideas into old men's heads' and that pioneers such as himself 'often held convictions which were unpopular with Authority, especially in the Navy.' Promoted to Commodore in 1915 (rather tardily in view of his responsibilities as Director of Airship Services) he was superseded by Rear Admiral C. L. Vaughan-Lee in the same year, to become Superintendent of Airship Production, on the pretext that he was 'overtaxed' by the job. In January 1916, although highly regarded by the younger generation of officers, he was posted to command blimp patrols in the Adriatic. Perhaps this was merely the Naval policy of keeping its people on the move, but it deprived the British Naval Airship Service of a pioneering and dedicated officer at the top. Denied a mainstream career by specialising in airships, he later left the Navy to become an M.P.

Sueter's contention that airshipmen had difficulty in making their ideas known, because they were low on the ladder of command, was borne out by wasteful patrol patterns dictated by commanders of surface ships who had failed to understand either the capabilities or limitations of the airship. For instance, a small blimp with a top speed of 50mph might be instructed to patrol downwind of an escorted force, giving it little chance of closing with a U-boat spotted to windward. The unfortunate pilot would later be taken to task for failure to keep station or respond to orders. As a young airship captain, T. P. York-Moore was ordered to patrol Mudros Harbour, Lemnos, where he spotted nine moored mines. From the ungracious response to this report he guessed that the base commander had 'planted' them in an attempt to prove that he would not see them and that therefore airships were useless. In fact, airships were able to spot mines easily in suitable conditions. Of course there were mistakes which could be used as ammunition by the critics, as when one pilot homed surface vessels onto the shadow of his own airship. There was also a captain who carefully stalked a trail of oil which had been laid by a drip from his own engine.

But apart from their deterrent value to U-boats, these small craft were able to scout ahead of the merchant ships and their escorts to look for hazards such as drifting mines, expended torpedoes or wreckage. This avoided the risky slowing down of convoys when suspicious objects were sighted ahead by surface patrols with a lesser field of vision.

Many surviving photographs of blimp operations suggest a tranquil and quite pleasant existence, far superior to being tossed about on the sea. But those images were taken on the good days, when a crewman had the energy (and warm enough hands) to operate a camera. For much of the time it was a miserable, bumpy and infinitely demanding occupation, requiring stamina and wakefulness over many hours. Modern jet travellers may find it difficult to visualise the hardship of sitting in an open cockpit with little protection from the weather, no hot food, no toilet facilities apart from a filler funnel and rubber tube. Even the aeroplane pilots of the day had their suffering limited by the known duration of flight - perhaps no more than two or three hours. The crew of an SS-Zero, with a theoretical endurance of 16 hours, could be in the air for as long as it took to see their convoy to safety. By reducing speed and prudent piloting the practical limit at 20mph could be extended to 40 hours. A conscientious pilot would often patrol for the duration of the useful daylight, returning to base in the dark to land by the light of paraffin flares or even a bonfire.

T. B. Williams, who flew the early SS ships from Anglesey over the Irish Sea, has described the task.

> As the pilot could not leave his little bucket seat during a flight of often many hours duration, he just didn't get a meal. He was the Captain of the airship, but if it was an SS, in addition to passing messages to and from his wireless operator, he had to read his maps and compass and take bearings and work out his course. He had to watch his instrument panel with all its clocks and gauges, including pressure, time, height, inclination, direction, and so on. He had to steer with his feet, ascend or descend by a wheel in his right hand; attend to engine and ballonet controls with his left hand; watch the ocean on all sides at all times; and when the crucial moment arrived, squint through his bomb sight, fuse his bombs and drop them! There were a few hangers on, also, such as the trail rope, grapnel, sea drogue, water ballast tank, all controlled by the pilot, though there were no parachutes in those days.
>
> (*Airship Pilot No.28* by Captain T. B. Williams AFC)

In the cramped and exposed conditions the cold would soon penetrate the heavy leather coat, woollens and thigh boots and the numbed crew might have to be lifted from their seats on landing. Some individuals were prone to airsickness, but even the strongest stomachs could be tried by a slow journey back to Howden over the Yorkshire Wolds on a windy day. Engine failure was a constant worry, resulting from broken or blocked fuel or oil pipes, overheating, cracked water jackets, contaminated fuel or magneto failure. Occasionally a coupling would break or a propeller fly off. The long control wires to rudder and elevators and ropes to gas and air valves were liable to snag or break, often leading to a forced landing. Over the land it might be possible to drop the trail rope to farm workers for attachment to a tree, otherwise a 'heavy' landing, possibly followed by deflation might be indicated. This latter manoeuvre was concluded by 'ripping' a panel on top of the envelope by means of a rope - inevitably requiring an explanation back at base. A forced landing at sea could be fatal unless a destroyer or trawler could take the sagging gasbag in tow while it still had some aerial buoyancy. Fifteen non-rigid airships were lost at sea during the Great War, although some of the crews were rescued. In addition, two *Coastals* were shot down by enemy floatplanes with the loss of their crews - C.17 off North Foreland on 21 April 1917 and

C.27 off Norfolk on 11 December 1917. C.25, which disappeared on a patrol from Longside, Aberdeen on 31 July 1918, is thought to have been hit by gunfire from a U-boat - a tactic later used in World War II against Coastal Command aircraft. The large non-rigid of the *North Sea Class*, NS.11, disappeared with its crew in July 1919, possibly due to being struck by lightning over the sea when on passage from Pulham, Norfolk, to Kingsnorth. At dawn on 22 July 1918, NS.3 met with disaster in stormy weather. Heading for base at East Fortune in a 40 knot wind, the ship suddenly lost height and dropped into the Firth of Forth at full speed, tearing off the engines and two engineers and damaging the envelope. The lightened but leaking remains then took off, with 8 of the 10 crew clinging to the car as it turned nose down before diving again into the sea. Captain Wheelwright and First Officer P. E. Maitland struggled onto the almost deflated envelope, where they were joined after a few minutes by the cox'n, one airgunner and one wireless operator. The other 5 were lost.

Fog was an additional hazard, although an airship had a better chance of survival than an aeroplane due to its slower speed. The *Coastal* C.11, flying from Howden, made landfall the hard way at Scarborough just two days after the loss of C.17. In thick fog the edge of the 500 feet hill known as Oliver's Mount tore off the rear part of the car, together with the engine and engineer, who landed on Scarborough Racecourse. Relieved of the weight the blimp rose rapidly, carrying the pilot (Sub-Lieutenant E. K. Hogg-Turnour) and the cox'n and wireless operator. Having lost his controls, including the valve lines, and fearing that the envelope might burst if the ascent continued, the pilot tried to ease the rip panel gently. The relative gas-to-air pressure was now so much that the panel ripped completely, dropping the ship out of control. The resulting crash broke both legs of the pilot and cox'n, and injured the wireless operator internally. It is probable that the latter died, but under the arbitrary censorship of the time the crash could not be reported in the press and later enquiries showed that no crash deaths were recorded in the area at that time. Hogg-Turnour returned to active flying and retired from the RAF as Captain in August 1919.

Airships were usually repairable, and the remains of C.11 were taken back to Howden and reassembled. Following a short test flight on 19 July 1917, she set off on a longer trial with a crew of six, piloted by Sub-Lieutenant Frank Harris, but less than an hour later she became very heavy and fell towards the River Humber opposite Brough, in spite of the release of all ballast and an attempt to fly dynamically at full throttle. Hitting the water at speed the car submerged, but not before the envelope had been torn and the gas ignited by one of the engines. Four of the crew were drowned. The two who survived owed their lives to Special Constable Frederick

Fig. 17 A Coastal Class non-rigid airship making a forced landing near Howden, with a landing party waiting to 'walk' it home.

Fig. 18 A Submarine Scout Zero blimp down in the sea after an engine failure. The crew are being rescued by boat.

Fig. 19 WRAF at Howden; Kathleen Appelbe is sixth from left, back row, 'Chiefy' Beautement is fourth from left, seated row.

Higham and his son Arthur, a Boy Scout of 15$^{1}/_{2}$ years. Seeing the airship in trouble, they followed it and then plunged into the uninviting and dangerous river to pull the shocked and barely conscious men to safety. Although news of the crash was restricted by the wartime obsession with security, father and son were presented with gold watches by the local Special Constables. Young Arthur Higham also received the Bronze Medal and Vellum of the Royal Humane Society.

Less likely to be fatal, but a common cause of damage, was the struggle to return a ship to its shed in a crosswind. In spite of the windshields which extended for several hundred feet beyond the doors, the envelope would buck and whip in the wind eddies which rolled over the barrier, sometimes lifting ground handlers off their feet and frequently damaging the control car or envelope. In fact several handlers did die through not letting go in time, though not at Howden. If difficulty was expected the entire personnel of the station would be called to General Assembly by bugle, the Petty Officers 'clearing the lower decks' by searching the barracks for evaders. In addition, if one of the *rigids* was to be brought out or rehoused, the local garrison at York would provide a few hundred soldiers. Even the WRNS (and later WRAF) were not exempt from landing and handling duties in emergency, which may have gone a long way towards the acceptance of women in this man's world. The nineteen year old Kathleen Appelbe and her friends had to abandon their lunch to land an airship on one occasion, and they were also mobilised for the labour-intensive task of rolling up the envelopes of deflated airships. Kathleen's presence at Howden may have been an indirect result of the tragedy of C.11, in which her boyfriend, Air Mechanic Harold Moore had drowned. The news was broken to her in Hull by Sergeant Gary Gurowich, another airshipman, and a friendship developed which was to draw her further into the lighter-than-air fraternity. Qualifying as a shorthand-typist, she joined the WRAF as an 'immobile' or home-based member, serving at Howden in the office of the Engineer Officer, Captain Seagram. In due course she married Sergeant Reginald Owen 'Gary' Gurowich. Women of the Women's Royal Naval Service and Women's Royal Air Force came to play a significant part in the work of the airship stations and aerodromes, engaging in more than 20 technical or semi-skilled trades, as well as the more conventional clerical, medical and domestic activities. Kathleen Appelbe was surprised to find an ex-schoolfriend 'on t'pigeons' as one of the two WRNS custodians of the pigeon loft - a back-up communication service which continued in Coastal Command into World War II. Airships and aeroplanes on long patrols would be issued with two pigeons in a basket, to be released in the event of radio failure or ditching. A pigeon could be launched in an open paper bag as protection from the slipstream during flight. It would then wriggle out and return to base.

It should be explained that the Women's Royal Air Force was formed on 1 April 1918, the day of the formation of the Royal Air Force. Volunteers were initially sought from the existing Women's Royal Naval Service and members of the Women's Auxiliary Army Corps (WAAC) who had been serving with the Royal Flying Corps. Later recruits were by direct entry, until by 1 April 1920, when it was disbanded, 32,000 women had served in the WRAF. In 1939 the service was reinstated as the Women's Auxiliary Air Force (WAAF) until 1949, when it again became WRAF.

Like any large service establishment, Howden had its own in-house social life, centred on the officers' and NCOs' messes and on the YMCA hut. Dances and amateur theatricals were occasions for letting down the hair and softening the formality of Naval protocol. They also brought guests to the camp by way of repaying the hospitality of the community. By these contacts and by the presence of the aerial sailors in local taverns a close bond was formed with the townspeople of Howden and its environs. Married personnel could 'live out' in lodgings in the neighbouring villages or farms. The two railways - the NER and the rival Hull and Barnsley Railway - gave easy access to Hull to the east and the industrial towns of Yorkshire to the west. As in a later war, York was a favoured destination for young airmen with a leave pass.

With so many men away in the trenches the presence of the airshipmen was a comfort to the young ladies of the district. It was a situation conducive to friendship, and many were the feet that found their way under hospitable tables - a traditional skill of servicemen. Thus it was that a number of girls married into the community of airship people, which because of its comparative smallness had an almost regimental affinity.

As in any service establishment, sport was encouraged, from team games to athletics. Certain enthusiasts, such as Lieutenant Carmichael Irwin, (later to die as the Captain of R.101 in 1930), might be seen in the early morning running around the airfield. Unable to indulge conveniently in water sports, some frustrated sailors built a land yacht with a large gaff rig in which they tacked across the landing ground in the evenings. More traditionally, a vacant airship shed invited the staging of a boxing tournament with ample accommodation for resident and visiting spectators.

Space was likewise not a problem out of doors, and with the arrival of a keen cricketing Chaplain, Revd Edwards, a pitch was laid out by volunteers on the north side of the approach road, opposite the already established football field.

With a ready supply of hydrogen and with the need to train more pilots, ballooning was available to willing candidates. This would involve a free ascent (that is, without being tethered) when the wind was favourable in strength and direction. On landing, the deflated envelope was packed inside the passenger basket and a farmer would be persuaded to take it to the nearest railway station. Thus Kathleen Appelbe received a telephone call from Air Mechanic Moore asking her to meet him at Hull Station, having just landed his balloon at Brough, near which he was later to die in C.11.

As the war progressed, it was thought advisable to institute parachute training for airshipmen, and this was undertaken from a moored balloon over the airfield, presided over at one time by the legendary Aircraftman 'Brainy' Dobbs, whose ingenuity and inventiveness had impressed the keen parachutist Edward Maitland. Dobbs was involved in many of Maitland's experiments with parachutes, and with the development of rubber boats. P. E. Maitland, survivor of NS.3 (no relation of Edward), remembered seeing Dobbs testing a prototype dingy made from gas tubing on the Medway at Kingsnorth.

The WRAF personnel at Howden lived in separate quarters which had been built near the Officers' Mess originally to house batmen. They were under the strict but benign control of Chief Section Leader ('Chiefy') Beautement. As their quarters backed on to open fields with New Plantation and Thompson's Plantation beyond she was not entirely successful in maintaining separation from the men. Being a countrywoman, and not much older than her charges, she may have turned a blind eye to the 'nature lovers' who would wander across the fields in the dusk carrying blankets. One of the perks of country life was the availability of fresh food, and the WRAF girls would take turns at collecting supplies from a local farm. On one occasion they had to wait until the butter was ready, and were delighted to discover a gramophone and records as they were keen on dancing to the new rhythms of the day. Hoping perhaps, to find 'Dardanella' or 'How ya gonna keep 'em down on the farm after they've seen Paree?', they were disappointed that the available discs were exclusively hymns; but by increasing the speed - easy enough on a wind-up gramophone - they were able to achieve a suitable dance tempo. At that time every service mess, canteen and ship had a gramophone - and even the rigid airships would have a Decca Model 1 'Trench' gramophone in the crew space with a supply of ragtimes, foxtrots and musical comedy numbers on 78 rpm shellac discs. It was expected that personnel returning from leave would bring back the latest musical comedy or dance records. In the pre-broadcasting days, popular music was disseminated by sheet music and the gramophone, as well as by music halls, theatres, concert parties and pierrot shows, and the orchestras and pianists of the 'silent' cinemas. The increasing popularity of dance bands was a consequence of the American presence in Europe during 1917-18, but also reflected the greater freedom gained by women through their war work.

At a time when every service recreational area had a piano, a pianist was assured of an audience and would not go thirsty. It is on record that some larger camps and battleships possessed player pianos (commonly known as *Pianolas*) but it is not known if Howden was so favoured. It is probable that the famous aluminium grand piano of the later *Hindenberg* is the only one to have flown.

However, it is a measure of the quietness and stability of rigid airship flight that the crew were able to enjoy the non-amplified strains of a portable gramophone.

With the coming of peace and the consequent relaxing of security, it was possible to welcome the public to service establishments. It was also desirable to enlist the pride and goodwill of the taxpayer for the continuance of funding. Thus it was that 140 members of the Hull Motor Cyclists Club were welcomed at Howden in April 1920, to be shown the giant airships R.32, R.33 and R.34 'in their mammoth hangers', formally expressing their thanks to the CO, Wing Commander Cunningham, and to Captain Oates and Lieutenant Moore 'for the conducted tour and explanations'.

VI

Mooring Out

Mooring out was just what it said - a blimp pegged down in the open air without benefit of one of the new sophisticated sheds, and very much at the mercy of wind and weather, particularly the wind. These advanced bases, sited near the coast, gave the advantage of reduced flying time to the patrol areas and thus extended the effective coverage of coastal shipping.

Life on a mooring-out station could be miserable or idyllic, depending not only on the weather but on the temperaments of the individual air and ground crews posted to them. Accommodation was usually in tents, with possibly a mess-hut or requisitioned building for daytime use. The more permanent members of the ground staff might find lodgings in the villages or farms, or at least be on regular visiting terms. For the blimps the commonest shelter was a clearing in a wood affording the space for one or two *Submarine Scouts*, with a narrow access corridor from the landing field through which the often fractious gasbag would have to be coaxed. Estates with Capability Brown style landscaping might offer ready-made nooks for airships to hide in; otherwise there was heavy work for a fatigue party or a welcome contract for a local sawmill. Inside the trees the wind was usually dissipated sufficiently to allow the envelope to be pegged down in safety, but getting it out for launching or returning it after flight was another matter. With half of the ship protected and the other half exposed to the wind there was serious risk of damage, as well as injury to the handlers. There was also the 'waterfall effect' of wind eddying over a belt of trees to torment a blimp moored in their lee. This happened to Captain George Meager's SSZ-55 at Kirkleatham near Redcar, a satellite station of Howden which was opened with scanty facilities in mid-1918. Secured by mooring guys to screw pickets, the ship surged up and down in the eddies and received sufficient damage to require a new car.

At the mooring-out stations, with a minimum complement of riggers and engineers, there was no recourse to a General Assembly summoned by bugler to land a ship. In some cases the returning pilot would decide to carry on to the parent station for a safe landing, invariably tired and also worried about fuel.

Hydrogen was supplied in cylinders for topping up but could not cope with a serious leakage, caused perhaps by a tear, and this would involve 'ripping' and the return of the complete airship to base for reinflating. Petrol, supplied in drums, had to be pumped by hand to tanks carried high in the envelope in fabric slings. Water ballast likewise would be pumped from a pond or lake. Loading bombs weighing up to 230 lbs was another call on muscular effort, as there was little in the nature of mechanical aids on the camp sites. It was hard work, with irregular hours and little chance for organised recreation, but had the compensations of relaxed discipline and pleasant surroundings. One of the American naval pilots operating from Lowthorpe, the main Howden satellite, described the site as a 'field of gold' on account of the carpet of buttercups. The clearing cut into Church Wood (then deciduous) looked its best in summer, but failed to hold one SS-Zero which broke away in a gale and travelled some distance before being arrested by a belt of trees. The station personnel were supplemented by a posse of volunteers from the nearby villages of Kilham, Harpham and Ruston Parva, and together they marched the truant home across the fields, thus avoiding the attention - and probable wrath - of Howden's 'Jimmy the One', Lieutenant-Commander Blatherwick.

This incident was typical of the close integration of the mooring-out stations into the rural scene in much the same way as dispersed sites on World War II airfields. The absence of service routine and protocol ('bull' in service argot) encouraged social contacts with the neighbours. Though at times a nuisance to farmers whose crops might be damaged during a forced landing or recovery operation, the airships and their people enlivened the sheltered but arduous life of the community. They were a particular delight to young boys like Harry Welburn and Norman Ulyott, who worked the fields near the landing ground at Lowthorpe. In the evenings and weekends they would hang around the camp and might on occasions be allowed to sit in one of the cockpits. Quite illegally, some villagers might be given short flights on a summer evening. There was an awkward occasion when local estate agent F. K. Hawes was on board an SS-Zero which fouled a tree, necessitating a report to the parent station. Fortunately he was uninjured and his presence was prudently not mentioned in the accident report.

A particular pleasure for young Master Robb was a ride in a motor cycle sidecar. Returning to his lodgings with the Harrisons in

Fig. 20 A Submarine Scout Zero (SS-Z) moored out in Church Wood, Lowthorpe.

Fig. 21 A Submarine Scout in trouble after breaking loose from its pickets.

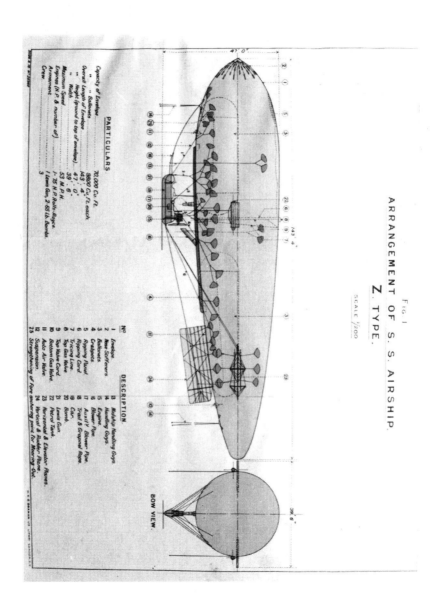

Fig. 22 Maintenance of the complicated rigging and controls was difficult at a mooring-out station.

Harpham village, Dispatch Rider A. R. Holloway would find the young man waiting breathlessly at the top of the hill, having run from the village on hearing the motor cycle leaving the camp.

One man who was not inconvenienced by the lack of organised sport was Captain Rainbow, who was recruited for the Harpham village football team during his service at Lowthorpe. On a more individual basis there was rabbit and pigeon shooting for those with landed friends, and it is not unlikely that a few pheasants went the same way. The fishing port and resort of Bridlington was only five miles to the east - an easy cycle ride - and fishing from the pier or inshore boats was possible even in wartime. In the westward direction the market town of Driffield offered a fair choice of hostelries and tea shops to connoisseurs of good Yorkshire cuisine and brewing, and was popular when a payday coincided with a spell of unflyable weather.

A circular pond with an artesian fountain, behind Lowthorpe Post Office, was a useful landmark for returning SS-Zeros. During the summer of 1918 it was also a popular rendezvous for some of the local young ladies. An informal airmail dating service developed by way of notes dropped to selected targets - further proof of the excellent scouting capabilities of the slow, low-flying blimps.

For the pilots, engineers and wireless operators, mooring-out could be an unsettling life, as they would frequently have to return to Howden with defective ships, to be treated as visitors or even intruders by the resident personnel. Travelling light, probably with little or no kit, they would have the aura of country cousins who had missed their bus home. Worse, as George Meager found, it could be difficult to muster technical assistance from petty officers with a 'base mentality'.

Airmen of a later war who have experienced diversions or detached service will know the feeling.

The mooring out stations, as well as the blimps they served, demonstrated the traditional ability of the Royal Navy (and later the Royal Air Force) to extemporise and to get on with the job with the available facilities. That this was done inside a notoriously brassbound organisation is a credit to the people who made it work, who not only risked their lives against the enemy and the elements, but were answerable to authority for errors. Fortunately in the 'paper war' which usually followed an accident, the mooring out stations were distant targets, and experienced campaigners became adept at writing reports and completing forms, thus dodging the 'friendly fire' of the bureaucrats.

Britain nearly lost the Great War to the U-boat. Its survival owed an incalculable debt to the *Submarine Scouts*, many of which worked from coastal mooring out sites. As a largely preventive force, they did not make the headlines or receive honour.

They won no great battles, but with their larger consorts - *Coastal, North Sea* and *Rigid* - they may have tipped the balance in the sea war.

VII

The Rigids

With two or three honourable exceptions, the British rigid airships made a poor comparison with the products of the Zeppelin and Schütte-Lanz companies. Coming late and hesitantly to airships, the Admiralty had difficulty in finding designers and constructors with any experience or even theoretical knowledge of aerostatics. For the few enthusiasts and the more numerous draftees to this branch of naval aviation, it was a matter of learning on the job, and picking up what tips they could by espionage and by examining the remains of grounded raiders. Consequently the British ships were based on German practice with a few rule of thumb modifications, and were several years out of date by the time they flew.

With some sort of logic, in that airships 'floated', the designers tended to come from ship or submarine design; but whereas the sizes were similar, the weights and stresses were vastly different. Also, with so few airships operational, British designers lacked the technical feedback which the German naval and army airship services provided, admittedly at some cost in lives and airships.

Considering these handicaps, credit must be given to the hundreds of men and women who built the giants, and to the handful of brave men who flew them. They too had to learn on the job. Their contributions to the science of flight have been obscured by some spectacular failures and by the relegation of lighter-than-air flight to a cul-de-sac in aviation history. Among their lesser known contributions were the development of navigational meteorology and pressure-pattern flying and the calibration of wind tunnel experiments by comparing models with full-scale measurements in flight. Even Concorde owes something to the experiments with R.29, R.32, R.33 and R.38, and modern jetliners are as conscious of weather patterns as the valiant and vulnerable R.34 in 1919; though the emphasis has shifted from mere survival to the commercial saving of fuel.

Possibly the greatest spin-off from airships to British aviation was the recruitment and development of Barnes Neville Wallis, who, after an apprenticeship in ship building, started as an assistant designer on the primitive No.9. With the pioneering Vickers designer H. B. Pratt, he was to be responsible for the detail design and modifications for five of the Zeppelin look-alikes which actually flew in wartime. The Admiralty design team (part of the Royal Corps of Naval Constructors) did not start work until July 1916, and only two of its designs (R.27 and R.29) saw war service.

As another part of his engineering education, B. N. Wallis became involved in experiments with duralumin (an alloy of aluminium and copper) which Vickers were carrying out for the Air Board. Apart from the wooden-framed Schütte-Lanz copies (R.31 and R.32) built by Short Brothers at Cardington, the British rigids were framed in this new alloy which was superior to the plain aluminium used in the earlier Zeppelins, but which required skilful heat treatment techniques. Thus the rather stumbling progress of British airship technology contributed to the later development of metal aeroplanes, in which Wallis was to play a leading part.

Barnes Wallis went on to design two original and successful airships (R.80 and R.100) and the remarkable *geodetic* Wellesley and Wellington aircraft, as well as conceiving the spectacular operation to breach the Ruhr dams in WWII. Later he contributed much to the development of supersonic flight.

HMA No.9 was built at Walney Island, Barrow, by the rather unwilling efforts of Vickers, who were as unsure as the Admiralty about the utility of airships and would have preferred to concentrate on their lucrative submarine and ship construction. After many stops and starts, No.9 hesitantly took the air on 27 November 1916, but it was not until 4 April the next year that she had been modified sufficiently to go to the Rigid Airship Trial Flight at Howden. Meanwhile young Barnes Wallis had made many friends among the RNAS personnel at Walney Island who were flying patrols over the Irish Sea or keeping an eye on the growth of No.9. Many of these acquaintances were to be renewed during his later career, notably the ebullient George Scott - then a blimp pilot but later to command R.34 on its Atlantic flight; also Flight Commander R. B. B. Colmore who became Director of Airship Development during the R.100/R.101 phase and who was to die with Scott in the latter ship in 1930.

While Wing Commander Masterman was fretting over the delays in the handing over of No.9, he applied his talents to the design of airship mooring gear which would simplify the handling of large dirigibles. He had already devised a mooring mast for blimps, and he now wished to do the same for the huge rigids, which normally required hundreds of handlers on the ground.

Fig. 23 No.9, the first British rigid dirigible to fly.

Fig. 24 With a panel of the envelope removed, riggers check the gasbag netting on No.9. This netting transmitted the lift from the gas cells to the hull framework.

Fig. 25 Mooring methods: R.34 on bridle mooring at Howden. It was the lack of a mast at Howden which finally wrecked the damaged R.34 and curtailed the training of the American airshipmen.

Fig. 26 R.33 on the Pulham mast.

Collaborating with young B. N. Wallis, he devised a system by which an airship could be reeled in and attached to a mooring pivot on a latticed mast. After tests with a 120 foot pylon, incorporating improvements suggested by George Scott, a mast was erected at Pulham for mooring experiments. Flight Lieutenant Pritchard, now recovered from the ravages of his Aegean service, and already recognised as one of the best airship brains, supervised many of these experiments. In this he was assisted by Flying Officer George Cook, later to take charge of the famous mooring tower at Cardington. Other masts were eventually constructed at Montreal, Ismailia and Karachi in anticipation of the proposed Imperial Airship Service.

However, No.9 was not to know the luxury of a tower at Howden, where outdoor mooring was to three wires attached to battleship anchor chains set in concrete. Obsolescent by the time she saw service, she was nevertheless a useful classroom for novice airshipmen who had never handled anything larger than a *Coastal* or *Parseval*. As first in the field, she bestowed some kudos on those who trained in her. Most of the later captains and cox'ns of British rigids had graduated in No.9 - aided by the handbook written by B. N. Wallis.

Apart from her didactic function, she was used for a variety of experiments both in the air and on the ground. Various mooring techniques were attempted, including riding to sea-drogues in the Wash. Handling trials showed a disappointing response to her rudders and a certain wilfulness about the direction of turn, with a preference for turning to port. She was finally damaged at Pulham during ground handling experiments with tractors and a converted tank and was broken up in June 1918, having flown for only 198 hours in total. However, she had taught her builders and operators a lot about rigid airships during her short life.

The next ships to emerge in the rigid series were known as the *23 Class*, and though an advance on No.9, they were some way behind the contemporary Zeppelins in performance. Designed by Pratt and Wallis at Vickers, only No.23 and R.26 (the first with the 'R' prefix) were built at Walney Island. In one of its periodic bursts of enthusiasm for airships, the Admiralty had coerced Beardmore's and Armstrong-Whitworth into building constructional stations. Hence No.24 was built at Inchinnan and No.25 at Barlow, Selby, to plans supplied by Vickers. The necessary interchange of expert staff between the various sites reinforced the 'extended family' nature of the airship community, which increasingly employed women as the trench war demanded more and more men. The skill and resilience of these women was recognised by the Admiralty Inspector at Barrow, who commented on the hardships of working in a shed with the doors left open for light, after standing for nine miles in a bus and walking half a mile to the shed.

In spite of the experience of the Barrow team, it was No.25 which won the race to Howden, arriving on 14 October 1917 from nearby Barlow. Next day she was joined by her Vickers-built sister No.23, which had been delayed by modifications to increase her useful lift. Neither of this pair saw much service, but continued the work of training and experiments with mooring methods. However, No.23 had the excitement of supervising the surrender of German U-boats at Harwich after the Armistice.

Predictably, together with their Scottish-built consort No.24, they attracted Admiralty displeasure due to unauthorised and allegedly dangerous modifications to their electrical systems by their crews. In defence of the men who were flying the ships, it was only by such pragmatic improvements that the development process was speeded up, as it would have taken months to have alterations authorised through official channels. Nevertheless, such irregularities must have given headaches to Major J. E. M. Pritchard, who as Admiralty representative was responsible for the test programmes of all new airships, and who as a trained mining engineer would be well aware of the hazards of electrical wiring in proximity to gas.

It should be made clear at this point that although the Vickers design and drawing office staff did most of the work, they were advised and supervised by resident and visiting Admiralty representatives. While this was legitimate, it frequently caused friction due to a conflict of ideas and to changes of mind by the Royal Corps of Naval Constructors who had nominal charge of airship building. That the changes were often for valid experiments (such as the carrying of aeroplanes for defence, tried out with No.23 and R.33) was small consolation to the hard-pressed designers and to the builders whose final payments were consequently delayed.

Of the rigids which saw service before the Armistice of November 1918, the most useful were in the *23X class* (R.27 and R.29), designed by Constructor-Commander C. I. R. Campbell of the Royal Corps of Naval Constructors. In spite of his submarine designing background, he created two robust and stable airships which were popular with crews. R.29, built by Armstrong at Barlow, was the only *rigid* to engage the enemy. Commissioned in June 1918 and operating from East Fortune, she sighted submarines on three occasions in her patrol area. One escaped; the second was thought to have hit a mine while fleeing; but it was third time lucky for her captain, Major G. M. Thomas. On 29 September 1918, noticing a faint trace of oil off Newbeggin Point, he summoned help by Aldis lamp from some surface vessels before dropping a 230 lb bomb on the oil slick. This was followed by depth charge attacks by the destroyers

HMS Ouse and *HMS Star* and two armed trawlers, with a further bomb from R.29. As oil continued to rise for the next few hours, it was assumed that the U-boat was mortally wounded. It was later deduced to have been UB-115. Major Thomas was awarded the DFC.

R.27 was not so lucky. Also commissioned in June 1918, she was stationed at Howden where she shared the No.1 Rigid Shed with three SS-Z blimps. On 16 August 1918, a US Naval crew who had been operating at Lowthorpe brought SSZ.23 in for a new envelope, in preparation for its shipment to the United States. As a goodwill gesture they fitted the old envelope to a spare car as a leaving present for their hosts. During the reassembly, petrol leaked into the bilges of the boat-shaped car and it was ignited either by a blowlamp or a spark from the radio transmitter under test. Two of the adjacent blimps exploded, followed in sequence by the eighteen gas cells of R.27. Amazingly, only one man - the lookout on the shed roof - was killed, but one US serviceman recalled being urged out of the shed by the successive puffs of hot gas.

Coming so close to the end of hostilities, the loss was not serious, but it was bad news for the wooden-framed R.31. With her sister R.32, she was the outcome of collaboration between the Admiralty team and a shadowy Swiss gentleman named Müller, who had arrived with detailed plans of the German Schütte-Lanz airships. Short Brothers, who were anxious to get into the airship business, were persuaded to take on the unusual construction. It was the birth of Cardington, as Short Brothers erected the first shed and the associated workshops and the living accommodation which is still known as Shortstown. The design work was slow, as sample girders had to be made and tested, and there was delay in obtaining the waterproof *Kalt Leim* glue used in the Schütte-Lanz ships. With a length of 615 feet and a diameter of $65^1/_2$ feet they were the biggest British airships of their time. When R.31 flew in August and October of 1918 she was found to have structural weaknesses and it was not until 6 November - five days before the Armistice - that she was posted to East Fortune. She never reached it, cracking girders forcing her to land at Howden where she was put to bed in the fire damaged No.1 Shed. Here she lay forgotten while the country celebrated the Peace and the Yorkshire winter rain poured through the roof to the detriment of her supposedly waterproof glue.

As she was now beyond repair, a Court of Inquiry was convened to 'apportion blame if any', but failed to find a scapegoat. R.31 was broken up after only nine hours flying. Her fabric was rolled up by the WRAF - recalled as backbreaking work many years later by Kathleen Appelbe - and sent off by rail to Cardington, while her delicate timbers were sold to a fuel merchant as kindling wood. Howden folklore has it that the wood was fireproofed!

Her sister ship, R.32, had a slightly longer and more interesting life. Commissioned on 3 September 1919, she was a well-liked and good tempered craft, and was one of the ships used for numerous experiments to determine the aerodynamic stresses on airship control surfaces and to equate these to wind-tunnel tests with models. Mr Pannell of the National Physical Laboratory, with an assistant (usually Frazer or Bateman) would be summoned at short notice to Howden or Pulham, where they would hurriedly connect up their manometers to the tubes in the fins ready for a start at first light. While Pannell ordered and recorded the helm conditions, Bateman or Frazer would note the manometer readings with a cine camera, continuing earlier work on R.29. Unlike R.31 she did not break but would bend visibly during a turn. She played her part in training US Naval crews of the Howden Detachment in 1920-21 (see Chapter 9).

In April 1921 she was stripped down to her underwear and used to test the effect of over-inflated gasbags. She was then broken up at Howden, to the regret of crews who had enjoyed flying in her.

With the coming of the Armistice the Howden airship boom was over. The future was uncertain for the airship people, but for the regulars (now in the Royal Air Force since the merger on 1 April 1918) there was the alternative of heavier-than-air flight, to which they were expected to transfer when their promotion became due. As the 'hostilities only' personnel were sent home and the outstations were closed, it was demoralising for the survivors to be running down the stores and dismantling airships. With their future employment in doubt it was not reassuring to mix with unemployed ex-servicemen in the surrounding towns. A fortunate few of the latter, like ex-tankman William Joy, were taken on as civilian workers at the airfield to supplement the depleted staff. Some business was provided by the arrival and testing of the rigids which were still emerging from the builders pending a decision about their future. As a symbol of hope, the enormous No.2 Twin Rigid Shed was still growing on the landscape, and was completed in April 1919.

Although the U-boats were now safely tethered in 'trots' in various estuaries, the residual menace of minefields had to be dealt with, and Howden's airships were kept busy directing surface craft to mines detected from the air.

For the regular airshipmen there was the interest provided by the new rigids R.33 and R.34 which were virtually copies of the Zeppelin L.33, forced down reasonably intact at Little Wigborough, Essex, on 24 September 1916. The Yorkshire built R.33, which had her first flight from Barlow within sight of Howden on 6 March 1919, was to become the longest serving British airship. She was used for many experiments including the carrying of defensive aircraft, for regulating road traffic on race days, and for mooring trials. She made history - and heroes of her captain Flight Lieutenant R. S. Booth and a skeleton 'anchor watch' - when she broke away from the Pulham mast in a storm on 17 April 1925, sustaining considerable damage to the bow and one gasbag. After a long struggle against the gale, she was nursed back to Pulham after about thirty hours, where the entire village turned out to land her. She was eventually repaired, and was not dismantled until 1928. She was used extensively on the pressure tests in flight for the calibration of wind tunnel models, following the work on R.29, R.32 and R.38. She was also registered as a civil ship (G-FAAG) for proposed passenger carrying trials.

Her twin sister, R.34, had a much shorter but eventful life. First flown from Beardmore's Inchinnan works on 14 March 1919, she was delivered to East Fortune on 30 May for crew training. This included a Baltic flight of 56 hours on 17-20 June as a reminder to the Germans that the Peace Treaty had not yet been ratified. With this meagre introduction to long distance flying, this airship was chosen for the ambitious project of an Atlantic crossing, under the command of Major George Scott, RAF, by now one of the most skilful and experienced airship pilots in Britain. With a lack of intermediate bases and no experienced ground crew at the destination, it was stretching R.34's luck to the limit, but the possibility of trans-Atlantic flight was exciting public and official interest and several contenders were already lined up. They included flying boats, landplanes and small airships, but R.34 would demonstrate the passenger carrying potential of the large dirigible. In fact she was not modified for passengers, but for prestige purposes she carried the redoubtable Brigadier General Edward Maitland, RAF, and Lieutenant Commander Zachary Lansdowne of the United States Navy. Major J. E. M. Pritchard, RAF, represented the Admiralty and was also the photographer. As the weather would be a vital factor, Meteorological Officer Lieutenant G. Harris was part of the crew, and it was hoped to maintain constant wireless contact with shore stations and ships.

Very few concessions were made to comfort, apart from a slightly enlarged crew platform with some tables and wash-basins. Hammocks were slung alongside the keel walkway, with a trapeze above each to ease the occupant in and out. Hot food was provided by boiling a saucepan on a plate welded to an engine exhaust. In these crude conditions it was planned to transport thirty men across a notoriously weather-fickle ocean, where every change in temperature and atmospheric pressure could affect the buoyancy of the ship - and hence its fuel consumption and speed as it resorted to *dynamic* flight.

It is not intended to tell the story in detail here as it has been adequately documented by many authors, including Maitland. (One of the best accounts is in *Airship*, by Patrick Abbott, 1973.) However, as R.34 provided such strong arguments to the airship lobby and was to influence policy, it is necessary to outline the achievement.

R.34 left East Fortune in the early hours of 2 July 1919, flying 'heavy' with the maximum load of fuel, one stowaway and the ship's cat. One hundred and eight hours later, on 6 July, with virtually no fuel left, she reached Mineola, Long Island, USA. As the landing party assembled by the US Naval Air Service had no previous experience of large rigids, it was decided to drop Major Pritchard by parachute to advise Lieutenant Hoyt, USN, in charge of the landing party. After a quick shave in hot water from an engine radiator he made the descent in full uniform to the delight of the spectators and newsmen. Soon the landing guys were safely in the hands of the ground crew, and the huge ship was picketed down. There followed a few exhausting days of formalities and celebration for some; hard work on the ship for others: until on 10 July she lifted off for the return flight. This time she did not carry the stowaway, AC2 William Ballantyne, who returned by sea. Ballantyne had been disappointed to be dropped from the crew to make room for the passengers, and had slipped on board during loading at East Fortune. Discovered after some hours, he was put to work (including the traditional fatigue of peeling potatoes) and his fate was deferred until arrival. The American press made something of a hero of him and he was photographed with the ship's cat, his fellow stowaway. He escaped serious punishment by the benevolence of Maitland and Scott, but not before he was reminded that his weight in petrol would have been worth twenty minutes of flying time. He continued in the RAF into the Second World War, qualifying as a pilot and ending as a Flight Lieutenant.

R.34 did not achieve the first Atlantic crossing, being beaten by three weeks by Alcock and Brown in a converted Vickers Vimy Bomber, but she did make the first - and more difficult - east to west crossing, and the first return flight. In spite of this achievement and its implications for air travel, R.34 and her courageous crew returned to a muted welcome, deliberately played down by an Air Ministry plagued by indecision about the future of airships. During the return flight Major Scott received instructions by wireless to divert to Pulham, thus avoiding the enthusiastic welcome and publicity which awaited at East Fortune. There was an official welcome of sorts, and telegrams from King George V and Prime Minister Lloyd George, but the moment had been spoiled. In a not inappropriate gesture, some of the forward water ballast was discharged on the heads of the band which was playing 'See the Conquering Hero Comes.'

Although the press in both Europe and America were predicting a great future for trans-oceanic airship travel, there was little official recognition for the airshipmen. John Alcock and Arthur Whitten-Brown had a few weeks earlier earned knighthoods for their marginal Atlantic triumph by aeroplane, which finished in an Irish bog. There were no R.34 knighthoods - merely four AFC's and a CMG for Scott, who already had the AFC for wartime service.

The subsequent history of R.34 is an anti-climax, but she had started something, and her fame, at least in USA, was to urge that country to a programme of rigid airship buying and building. Meanwhile, following her Atlantic adventure she was returned to East Fortune for a lengthy refit, and after another brief stay at Pulham she was posted to Howden in March 1920 for crew training in company with the popular R.32. As a flying classroom she had the advantages of space for extra crewmen and endurance for extended training. In particular she was useful for navigation and wireless instruction as she could remain airborne at nights and cover considerable distances.

It was in this capacity that R.34 set off from Howden at noon on 27 January 1921, captained by Flight Lieutenant Hedley Drew and a 'class' of eight navigators. Perhaps a more experienced and closely knit crew would have avoided the follies which now followed, but Drew had but recently taken over command of R.34 and he was unfamiliar with the local geography. In an oversight familiar to generations of navigators by land, sea and air, his charts were out of date. In particular they did not show the recently amended flashing codes for lighthouses and buoys. A gremlin had also entered the wireless cabin, and not only was the ship transmitting on an incorrect wavelength, but the senior wireless operator had been given the wrong call sign by Howden. In consequence, Howden could not receive R.34's transmissions and R.34 assumed that recall signals which *she* received were in fact for R.32.

By the time that the truth dawned, R.34 was well out to sea in worsening weather and it was getting dark. A conference of the captain, officers and eight navigators placed the ship off Spurn Head and on this assumption a course was set along the supposed Humber towards Howden. Not entirely convinced by the navigator's calculations, Drew descended carefully through the cloud and rain in search of a landmark. Shortly after midnight the control car and the forward and aft engines hit the North York Moors, many miles north of the supposed position, with the loss of two propellers. There was no alternative but to drop ballast, start the two remaining engines, and wait over the sea until daylight for a visual fix. After a tedious crawl along the Humber against a strong wind, Howden was reached just before dark and R.34 was taken hold of by 400 ground handlers. Surging and buffeting in the rising wind, she was walked to the shed but proved unmanageable in spite of the windscreens leading to the doors. Fearing casualties, Air Commodore Maitland (now CO of Howden) ordered the crew to leave the ship. Bouncing and crashing to the peril of the handlers, she was walked to the three-wire mooring point by the Spaldington Road and tied down for the night. By the morning she was badly damaged forward and settling on the ground. There was no alternative but to dismantle her where she lay - a sad end to a gallant and well-liked airship.

The inevitable Court of Inquiry, unable to 'apportion blame' to its satisfaction, was obliged to arbitrarily distribute reprimands to Maitland, Drew and the Senior Flying Officer, Flight Lieutenant Wann.

Two points emerged from the accident to R.34. Firstly, it showed the vulnerability of a giant rigid airship on the ground in bad weather. If R.34 had been modified for mast mooring, like her sister R.33, she could have been landed to the Pulham mast even in her damaged condition. In fact she had been partly modified but was awaiting the mooring nose-cone. It had been proposed to build a mast at Howden, but this was also delayed pending a decision about the future of airships in Britain.

The second point is that R.34 never killed anyone, in spite of colliding with a Yorkshire hilltop in the dark. In an aeroplane, this would almost certainly have been fatal. It was the apparent safety of airships of that period (in comparison with aeroplanes) which encouraged their proponents to carry on. There was also the advantage of extended flight, which made them very suitable for maritime patrol work as well as commercial passenger carrying.

For the United States of America - already enthusiastic users of non-rigid airships and now emerging as a world power - the rigid dirigible seemed an ideal component of an ocean-going navy, particularly in the vast Pacific. In addition, America had a natural source of inert helium to replace the highly inflammable hydrogen gas, so that this particular danger did not arise.

Deprived of a 'reparations' Zeppelin by the wrecking of the German airships by their crews in 1919, they had ordered a replacement from the Zeppelin Company, to be paid for by the German people. They had also commenced to build one at home and had negotiated the purchase of R.38 - the latest and greatest British design and at that time the largest airship in the world. Under construction at the Royal Airship Works, Cardington, she would become ZR-2 of the United States Navy. As part of the deal, a party of US Naval airshipmen were sent for training at Howden, Pulham and Cardington. They were known collectively as the *Howden Detachment*.

VIII

R.38 - The Unwanted Child

Whether it is due to insecurity and unwillingness to be committed to a specific course, or to an open-minded policy of trying all the options, compromise seems to be a basic British instinct - an advantage at times, but a fatal eroder of policy and decision-making when large issues are at stake. The Admiralty's approach to the naval rigid airship programme was a series of compromises between the conflicting interests of traditionalists and innovators, planners and builders, servicemen and politicians; with the Treasury always poised to veto expenditure. Whether the result of too many committees, too little money or too many protagonists, compromise troubled not only the arguments about the need for naval airships but also the methods of designing and building them.

The coercing of Vickers, Beardmore and Armstrong into the rigid airship programme was a distasteful necessity in the race against the Zeppelin, as the Admiralty would dearly have liked to have gone it alone. Having made these sordid commercial arrangements they were not content to let their contractors get on with it. As the major builders, the Vickers airship team were particularly plagued by the demands of the Corps of Naval Constructors, leading to modifications, delays and many returns to the drawing board by Pratt and Wallis.

Short Brothers, who got their chance through the fortuitous arrival of Herr Müller with the Shütte-Lanz blueprints, were soon to regret their involvement. With the ending of the war and the completion of the wooden twins, R.31 and R.32, the Admiralty decided to assert itself. Given brief notice, the Short Brothers' Cardington establishment was nationalised to become the Royal Airship Works - analogous to a Royal Dockyard, with Constructor-Commander Campbell as Manager as well as Chief Designer. Short Brothers' interest was bought out with nominal compensation. At last the Airship branch of the Corps of Naval Constructors had a place of its own, and could put a newly-found confidence to work.

Towards the end of the war, helped in no small way by the examination of downed Zeppelins, the Admiralty team had at last felt capable of pressing ahead of the German designs. The result was to be the 'A' class; the biggest, fastest, highest-flying naval scouting dirigible in the world. Abandoning R.37, the last of the modified '33' class still on the stocks at Cardington, they laid down R.38 alongside it, imposing their will on the captive Shorts' personnel. Bold decisions do not always lead to easy solutions, and forces both inside and external to Cardington were to trouble the history of R.38, not least the uncertainty of continued employment of the workforce. For example, the initial contract with Shorts was placed in September 1918, but this was cancelled on 31 January 1919 and then reinstated on 17 February. The huge unfinished skeleton of R.37 was a constant reminder of possible redundancy, even as work on R.38 progressed. That the internal difficulties were overcome is a tribute to the designers and builders. The external factors - political, financial, international - were to set the airship on a course of no return, and to lead inevitably to disaster.

The truth was that R.38 had acquired the status of an unwanted child. Conceived in wartime, it narrowly escaped being aborted as a peacetime economy measure. Winston Churchill, as Secretary of State for Air in 1919, was violently opposed to airships and recommended cancellation, particularly as they had been transferred from Admiralty to Air Ministry control on 22 October 1919. Orphaned before birth by the demise of the RNAS, briefly fostered by the RAF, it survived only by the promise of adoption by the United States Navy.

The specification, which had been arrived at with North Sea service in mind, called for a combination of high speed and the maximum possible ceiling, mainly as a defence against attacking aircraft. At this time, in spite of increasing successes by British aeroplanes against the Zeppelins, an alert airship captain could escape by dropping bombs and ballast and rapidly ascending out of reach of his tormentors. It seemed prudent to build this attribute into the new design, and 22,000 feet would put it out of reach of most intercepting aircraft then in service. In addition, a scouting dirigible for North Sea service would require an endurance of six days at a range of 300 miles from base. Even at its top speed of 70mph it should be capable of 65 hours of flight. These requirements suggested a ship of 3,000,000 cubic feet gas capacity and a length of 750 feet; but because of shed limitations, a compromise of 2,724,000 and 699 feet was arrived at, with a diameter of 85.5 feet dictated by the roof clearance of the Cardington shed. A much larger facility, at

Flookborough in Lancashire and intended for Vickers, had been cancelled before completion at the end of the war. The Cardington shed was later heightened and lengthened for the building of R.101, and a second shed was brought from Pulham and enlarged to house R.100. Meanwhile the R.38 designers had to make the best use of the available space.

To understand why R.38 had such a difficult gestation we must consider the difficulties faced by the design team. The expectations for a new 'A' type dirigible were very ambitious, beyond anything achieved by the best of the Zeppelins to date. The *specification* having been settled after much wrangling between the operational, constructional and planning teams, the initial design was formulated in consultation between the Admiralty Airship Design Department, led by C. I. R. Campbell, and Short Brothers' design office at Cardington. Campbell's department developed the overall design (i.e. shape, dimensions, girder sizes, number of gas cells, engines, stressing, etc.) and Short Brothers produced the working drawings. Sister ships R.39, R.40 and R.41, slightly shrunk to fit the available sheds, were to be built by Beardmore and Armstrong Whitworth, and *at least* two of these were laid down at Inchinnan (Clydeside) and Barlow (Selby). There is confusion about this because of orders, cancellations, reorders and final cancellation of all except R.38, which possibly inherited some parts originally made for her sisters.

The process of nationalising the Cardington factory dragged on for months with neither designers nor workers knowing what their future would be in the Royal Airship Works. When Campbell became Manager of RAW he had no option but to retain the services of Shorts' drawing office staff headed by C. T. P. Lipscomb. There was no shortage of advice from interested parties, but those who might be regarded as 'expert' by virtue of experience were usually junior in rank (aviation being a very recent science) and their opinions were often ignored or rejected. In fact, they were inclined to be regarded as troublesome, especially by traditionalist non-flying naval officers.

This seems to have been the fate of Wing Captain E. A. D. Masterman, one of the earliest Royal Navy aviators and an enthusiastic exponent of lighter-than-air flight. As early as 1916 he had proposed an Admiralty airship works, to be sited at Lough Neagh in Northern Ireland. Unfortunately he was tainted, in Admiralty eyes, by associations with Vickers, pioneer builders of British rigid airships as well as warships. As head of the Royal Navy's Rigid Trial Staff he took delivery of the Barrow-built airships, and was much respected by their designers H. B. Pratt and B. N. Wallis. As the Admiralty had frequent disputes with Vickers, Masterman appears to have been regarded with some suspicion by authority. By those better able to judge, he was acknowledged as one of the best brains in the wartime Airship Service, but surprisingly, he transferred to the Army as a Brigadier General when the RAF was formed on 1 April 1918. Presumably this was due to frustration, as he had been a strong advocate of a bolder wartime airship programme. It will be recalled that it was he and Barnes Wallis of Vickers who had designed the first practical airship mooring mast, erected at Pulham Airship Station in Norfolk.

Understandably, after the Armistice there was no help from the Zeppelin Company (Luftschiffbau Zeppelin) who wished to develop long range commercial passenger flying and were smarting under the provisions of the Peace Treaty which banned them from manufacturing aircraft parts and from flying airships. Masterman, who was a member of the Control Commission enforcing the rules, received an angry letter from Zeppelin's general manager threatening to destroy all remaining airships if the ban continued. *No way* were they going to help a potential rival.

Likewise it was unrealistic to expect help from the competing and now disgruntled British contractors (Armstrong Whitworth, Beardmore, Vickers) who were not only left with partly completed airships, meagre compensation and redundant workers, but were excluded from future design developments by the RAW monopoly.

As for scientific data, there had been only limited experiments to date and not much was known about aerodynamic forces on large airships. The Germans had built their *height climbers* in desperation to escape attack, and then largely by trial and error. The British could design *warships* where weight was of secondary consequence and safety factors (*factors of ignorance* in engineering jargon) could allow for unknown stresses. It was different facing the unknown when doubling a safety factor could mean doubling the weight and thus reducing the useful lift of an *airship*. At least four of the airship designers had previously worked on submarines, including Campbell, and while there were similar problems of balance and buoyancy between submarines and airships, the stresses were of a totally different nature.

At the inquiry after the R.38 crash it was revealed that some National Physical Laboratory research, a French report on airship experiments and a report from a British team which examined Zeppelins after the Armistice had been available during the later design stages of R.38. Through some bureaucratic muddle they did not seem to have reached the RAW design team - or not early enough to influence the basic structural design.

That the aerodynamic test results were too little and too late was not due to any lack of diligence by the National Physical Laboratory staff, who had been asked late in 1918 to investigate the effects of

Fig. 27 Constructor-Commander Campbell, Designer of R.38 (3rd from left) with
Sir Frederick Sykes, Controller-General of Civil Aviation on his right
and Commander Dyer, USN, on his left.

Fig. 28 A main frame of sister ship R.39 under construction at Armstrong Whitworth's Barlow Works. When R.39, R.40 and R.41 were cancelled, their completed parts were said to have been used for R.38.

Fig. 29 The distinctive framing of R.38 with one gas cell in place. The braced main frames with two unbraced intermediates are clearly visible, and the transverse bracing wires are outlined against the gas cell.

Fig. 30 The bow of R.38 showing the mooring cone, mooring hatch and the outline of the gangway for access to the tower.

rudder movements in large rigid airships for correlation with wind tunnel tests. The trials - in several senses - of Mr J. R. Pannell, the senior NPL airship aerodynamicist, and his assistants will illustrate the difficulties. Owing to the restricted peacetime flying programme they might be notified on a Saturday night that they could fly on Sunday morning in R.26, R.27, R.32 or R.33. Packing their instruments in a car, they would dash to Pulham or Howden, install the equipment and snatch a few hours of rest before takeoff in the calm air of early morning. The tests were incidental to the main purpose of the flight and would be fitted in as convenient, assisted usually by Captain George Meager, an experienced wartime airship officer. The work was fatiguing and frustrating, as the flights were sometimes for the instruction or pleasure of members of Parliament or other VIP's whose commitments influenced the route, timing and duration of flight. Captain Meager gives us a glimpse of the conscientious 'Mr Pannell of sliding fame' - this either a pun on his name by irreverent airmen or a reference to his frequent use of the slide rule. He was 6'4" tall, with 'a huge head and body frame'. One or more of his NPL colleagues (Frazer, Simmons, Duffield or Bateman) would accompany him on the test flights, and Captain Meager's demobilisation was postponed for six weeks to complete the series. With the courage and dedication of the true scientist and in the certain knowledge of R.38's vulnerability the redoubtable Mr Pannell planned to continue the experiments in the completed airship.

Delay in completing R.33 and R.34 - based on the Zeppelin L.33 brought down at Little Wigborough, Essex - and R.36 which incorporated improvements found in two other Zeppelin casualties (L.48 and L.49), meant that they had not even flown before R.38 was designed. If they had, they might have provided early warning of the fragility of the *height climber* framework. All three of these Zeppelin look-alikes later suffered structural damage in flight or during handling, but more significantly they each experienced extreme weather conditions which could have suggested the need for generous factors of safety in calculating the strength of girders.

It is likely that the recovery of parts of L.70 from the sea further misled the British designers. This Zeppelin, of the latest height-climbing pattern, was shot down off the Norfolk coast on 6 August 1918 by Major Egbert Cadbury and Captain Robert Leckie in a DH4 aircraft. It had fallen close to the schooner *Amethyst* in shallow water and was easily located by Royal Naval salvors. With minimum weight as the main design criterion it was as fine boned as an aircraft could be, and required to be flown with great delicacy. As the salvaged parts were not accompanied by an instruction book, this operational limitation may not have been appreciated by the R.38

team during the early, crucial design stages. The fact that Fregattenkapitän Peter Strasser, Leader of Airships, had been aboard L.70 may have emphasised that this was the last word in Zeppelin technology.

The crosscurrents in the British airship programme (eg. commercial versus state constructors, civil versus military aviation, aeroplanes versus airships, Admiralty versus Air Ministry, development versus economy, professionals versus politicians) not only affected builders and airshipmen, but gave Campbell and his small team much extra work and worry. As each new proposal was agreed by the planners, he would have to produce a design which might reach the building stage only to be cancelled or modified on the stocks. This partly explains the strange gaps in numbering of British rigid airships. To this was added the new distraction of managing the nationalised Royal Airship Works.

The craft which gradually took shape in the huge shed at Cardington, alongside the abandoned skeleton of R.37, was basically a Zeppelin in form and structure but with a number of new and untried features. To reduce weight the number of gas cells was reduced to 14 (against 16 to 20 bags in contemporary rigids) as large bags gave a better volume-to-surface-area ratio. This meant that the bays which housed the gas cells between the main transverse frames would be longer than normal, with two instead of one intermediate rings, unbraced transversely. This also saved weight, but it meant longer diagonal bracing wires between frames, and longer unsupported sections of keel. The later Zeppelin practice of using stirrup wires from frames to keel was not used, and the 50 petrol tanks were hung directly from the main frames instead of being dispersed along the keel, as was usual. Instead of the normal use of hemp netting to enclose the gas bags and transfer their lift to the hull framework, a system of circumferential wires and longitudinal catenaries was used. The keel corridor was trapezoid in section - a less rigid form laterally than the conventional triangle.

Like a growing cuckoo, R.38 was not comfortable in its inadequate nest, and this had influenced its shape and its ultimate strength. Due to height limitations in the shed it had been necessary to include two parallel sections in its length, immediately robbing it of the potential resistance to bending which a chubbier shape would have contributed. Of the six engines, the two midship cars were placed high on each side to reduce the overall height of the airship. Because of the slender attachment struts and the fragile nature of the hull framework, thrust wires were run from the front and rear of each car to the main frames, the rear wires being attached to bearings in the hubs of the pusher airscrews. The engines being further than usual from the centreline with its comparatively rigid keel not only complicated the attachment to the hull, but could also induce imbalanced lateral bending moments during turning.

One significant American requirement was the installation of mast mooring gear which involved also reinforcement of the bow and added a ton to the weight. To restore the balance, a ton of extra water ballast was provided at the stern, reducing the useful lift and inducing a slight *hogging* of the structure. As this put the upper longitudinals in tension (the substantial keel taking the compression) it was nothing to worry Campbell, as the delicate girders were safer in that condition. He seems to have overlooked the possibility that the straining wires from the engine cars might put those longitudinals immediately forward of their attachment points into dangerous compression.

So many innovations, so little scientific data, so many conflicting requirements. Regarding the latter, no one seems to have considered changing the basic specification to meet the *American* operating requirements, which would not entail such a high ceiling, there being little prospect of aircraft attack in the Pacific or Western Atlantic at that time. As the sale was agreed in October 1919 with the construction not very far advanced, there would have been time to incorporate modifications. Perhaps it was the US Navy pressing for a speedy completion, or the British haste to be rid of military airships which ruled out any rethinking. It is more likely that neither party was eager to pay for alterations, and did Britain have the spare girders from the cancelled sister ships R.39 and R.40 (and R.41?) to use up?

Whatever the reasons there was now an incentive at Government level to finish the construction without delay, but this was probably not shared by the builders (ex-Short Brothers) who would be working themselves to redundancy. They lived in the small estate named Shortstown behind the airfield complex, and like all skilled craftsmen they were a close community. While not suggesting that they deliberately dragged their feet, they must have been demoralised by the insecurity of employment and the stop-start nature of airship construction to date. The ghostly frame of R.37 was alongside them as they worked - a sort of airship *memento mori*. For the record, a large number of the workforce were women, so that airship construction was very much a community experience. As one former fabric worker put it, with nostalgia and pride, 'We were just like brothers and sisters'.

IX

The Howden Detachment

The first draft of the US Naval Rigid Airship Detachment arrived at Howden on 20 April 1920. It comprised nine officers and eighteen enlisted men, and included a Medical Officer and a Supply Officer, the latter presumably to deal with the paperwork without which no military organisation can function. The officer in charge, who was also the captain-designate of ZR-2, was Commander Louis Henry Maxfield, a qualified pilot of aeroplanes and airships and holder of the Navy Cross. Born in St. Paul, Minn, in November 1883, he was now 36 years old. One of the pioneers of US Naval Aviation, he had commanded the US Naval Air Station at Paimboeuf in 1917. After the war he had been the Lighter-than-Air Aide at the Office of Operations, Washington DC.

Perhaps reflecting the newness of rigid airship technology, Engineer Officer Lieutenant Commander Valentine N. Bieg had been transferred from the seagoing navy, in which he had seen wartime service in *USS Trippe* and the destroyer *USS Dent*. His new vessel was to be considerably larger though significantly more delicate than either of his previous ships.

In July a second draft of seven officers and eighteen men 'reported aboard', to be followed at intervals by another ten and a Meteorological Officer, Lieutenant J. B. Anderson. From time to time various supernumerary officers appeared, some of whom were to be passengers on the trans-Atlantic crossing. Of these, Lieutenant Richard E. Byrd, USN (Ret.), was to achieve later fame for his Polar exploration flights, but just now he was a frustrated man, having been thwarted in two previous US Naval attempts to cross the Atlantic. An experienced navigator, he had requested but been denied command of the flying boat NC-3, which with two consorts had planned to reach England by way of Newfoundland, the Azores and Lisbon in May 1919. As compensation he had flown as a

Fig. 31 Members of the USN Howden Detachment pose in their new flying suits. It would appear that only one size was available! (Photo: Winged Cobra Collection, Leeds)

Fig. 32 USN crewmen of the Howden Detachment pose with senior staff of the Royal Airship Works, Cardington.

Fig. 33 United States Naval officers receive instruction at Howden on R.34

passenger in NC-3 as far as Newfoundland, and had been offered a place on the non-rigid airship C-5, which was to make a separate bid. In the event, NC-3 was damaged in a landing at sea, and was only able to reach the Azores by running on the surface, NC-4 being the only one of the trio to complete the crossing. Meanwhile C-5 had broken away from its moorings during a storm on the eve of departure on 15 May, hastily abandoned by Lieutenant Charles G. Little and two enlisted men. Little broke a leg but survived to join the Howden Detachment. The thwarted Richard Byrd was to have one more disappointment when he missed the final flight of ZR-2 from Howden, but his frustration would have been of short duration. Charles Little did not miss this flight.

The vagrant C-5 caused even greater chagrin to Lieutenant Commander Emory Wilbur Coil, USN, who as captain of C-5 might have been the first to fly the Atlantic directly. Coil, graduating from Naval College in 1911, had learned to fly at Pensacola in 1916 and qualified as lighter-than-air pilot at Akron, Ohio, in 1917. He then commanded the Rockaway Naval Air Station before replacing Maxfield as the Lighter-than-Air Aide at Washington. A period as a member of the Allied Aeronautical Commission of Control (supervising the disarming of the defeated Germany) gave him experience of Zeppelin practice. In July 1920 he became the Executive Officer of the Howden Detachment - in effect Maxfield's deputy. Possibly because he had lost his mother and his wife to the influenza epidemic of 1918, and had no family ties, he left instructions for his burial at sea in the event of his death. Although he seems to have remarried (The New York Times reporting that his wife was with him in England), the request was left on the file.

With the exception of Bieg and the Publicity Officer Lieutenant Tinker, all the officers scheduled for the trans-Atlantic flight were qualified airship pilots. The enlisted men had also been chosen for their experience, mostly gained on non-rigid airships.

The Howden Detachment, earmarked for ZR-2 and her consorts-to-be, commenced their training on 21 April 1920, happily unaware of the delay and indecision which would plague the first of their new fleet of rigid dirigibles. They soon had problems of their own. They had been allocated R.32 (the Schütte-Lanz look-alike) for basic training and handling experience. For a time there was no hydrogen available to reinflate the twenty-one gas cells because of a shortage of coke for the hydrogen plant, so they stripped and refurbished the somewhat neglected ship until she was reinflated.

As a stopgap, the large non-rigid NS.7 of the North Sea Class and the sleek experimental blimp SSE.3 were spared from intended deletion until late 1920, so that some flying training could be commenced.

Although liked by her regular crews, the plywood-framed R.32 must have been unnerving for trainees in several ways. It was said that a crewman at one end of the keel corridor might see a colleague at the other end appearing and disappearing as the structure flexed in flight. There was also the haunting memory of sister-ship R.31 which had been broken up following girder failure, occasioned first in flight and then by softening of its casein glue during storage in Howden's leaking No.1 Shed. The leaks being due to a joint US/British accident which ignited R.27 and several blimps in August 1918 was a coincidence to be considered by the superstitious. Airship crews basically were sailors and shared their folk-lore.

Additionally, the fact that they were allowed *exclusive* use of R.32 could not have reassured those who knew that the Air Ministry considered the ship to be due for scrapping and therefore expendable. In fact she was dismantled at Howden in April 1921 at the tender age of twenty months.

Having enjoyed this hands-on experience they were now brought back to RAF control as students. The hard-working and conventional R.33 - a copy of the salvaged 'Little Wigborough' Zeppelin - had recently arrived at Howden for crew training and experimental flights. At least some of the American personnel were on board for instruction during June and July of 1920. Her glamorous sister R.34 was also in commission and it was promised that they could graduate on her later in the year. In 1919 R.34 had made aviation history by the first double crossing of the Atlantic by any aircraft, shortly after the one-way flight of Alcock and Brown in a Vickers Vimy bomber. As R.34 had been the object of much admiration and celebration on her arrival at Mineola, near New York, she had much more status for the US Navymen than the redundant and quirky R.32.

The euphoria was to be short-lived. As already recounted, during an RAF-manned training flight in January 1921, R.34 had scooped up heather and gorse from the North York moors at night, leaving two of her four propellers and other fragments in exchange. She had struggled back to Howden on two engines but could not be coaxed into her shed due to a rising cross-wind. There being no mooring mast at Howden she was tethered for the night to three-wire bridle on the open airfield. By the morning she had been buffeted beyond repair and was broken up where she lay.

The Howden Detachment was now allocated the small but highly efficient R.80, designed by Barnes Wallis of Vickers, but also due for deletion as an economy measure. The US Navy had considered her purchase, but had opted instead for the longer flight duration of the Admiralty 'A' design. In this well-behaved little ship they continued their flying training until the eventual arrival of R.38/ZR-2 from the Royal Airship Works.

From time to time some crew members visited Cardington for training in engineering aspects, and all were taken to Pulham to examine the Zeppelins L.64 and L.71. These two had escaped the airship equivalent of scuttling at the hands of German airshipmen, and had been surrendered to Britain under the Armistice terms, although they never flew again after arrival at Pulham.

They were also introduced to the prudent though stressful practice of parachuting from a moored balloon at Howden. Air Commodore Maitland's enthusiasm for this mode of descent may not have been shared by all British and American crewmen, but it was designed to save lives and there were parachutes for all on R.38. Although of the static-line type and not worn in flight, they were distributed around the crew stations - including the engine cars - ready to be clipped to the harness suits supplied to all crew and passengers. These suits of heavy canvas were cumbersome and uncomfortable, and were made by RAF personnel on the airship stations. An improved commercial version known as the *Parasuit* was available from Messrs. Robinson and Cleaver Ltd. at £7.5s. (£7.25) per outfit. As the first flight of R.38 approached it had still not been decided whether the RAF could afford the luxury of individually fitted *Parasuits* and whether the Americans would pay for their own or receive them as a free issue with the ship. Although the correspondence between the RAF, USN and Robinson Cleaver is now lost, it seems likely that the Americans had to make or buy their own suits or borrow from RAF spare crewmen.

In charge of parachute training was the legendary Aircraftman Ernest Arthur 'Brainy' Dobbs, held in awe for his many innovations and experiments but apparently ill-rewarded for his trouble. He was a dedicated collaborator in Maitland's trials, which included dropping dummies from airships and from the roof of the Cardington shed. It is not recorded whether his dog, which made a number of descents, shared his enthusiasm! Perhaps if Maitland had survived there would have been recognition of his contribution to life-saving technology, later to include inflatable dinghies.

Another enthusiastic exponent of the parachute was Major Pritchard, probably the only man to have arrived in America by this means. Having descended from R.34 at Mineola to assist the inexperienced landing party, he held the distinction of being the first east to west Atlantic air traveller. Now planning the R.38 flight trials, he again met Lieutenant Hoyt, who had been in charge of the Mineola handling party.

Life at Howden during the early stages of training could have been boring, as the rundown of the station had commenced, flying was limited, and many of the British servicemen (and women) had departed. In-house entertainment for the enlisted men was restricted to occasional dances and amateur theatricals, and it could be cold in the wooden barrack huts, to which a final bill for over £100 for barrack damages and deficiencies bears witness. Howden lies at the western end of the Humber Estuary, surrounded by meandering rivers, and subject alternately to fog and to winds which whistle unhindered across the flat ground. In summer it is pleasant enough, but work on airframes in necessarily unheated sheds is taxing in winter, especially on tall structures made slippery by freezing fog.

However, servicemen being what they are, they were soon at home in the neighbourhood; liked and respected by the hospitable Yorkshire people and welcome to 'put their feet under the table' in service parlance. Romances developed, some to flourish, some to fade. A later report in an American newspaper that US Naval personnel had to go about in pairs for mutual protection from a hostile population was pure and undeserved malice, much resented by those who had been directly involved with, or part of, the Howden Detachment.

Whether as a result of the coldness of the barracks or the warmth of their welcome, seven of the crewmen and one of the officers acquired British wives during their stay. Another man had married a Belgian girl, and some officers had brought their wives from the United States. By the second summer at Howden they were well established as guests of the community and enjoying the social life which develops around any Service establishment. This included an inter-service sports day, attended also by wives, fiancées and friends. Even Lieutenant Charles G. Little, who had been lucky to escape with a broken ankle from the runaway blimp C-5 in 1919, showed his confidence in the future by importing Miss Joy Bright from New Jersey to be his bride at Brough in October 1920. In the RAF contingent, Flight Lieutenant Godfrey Thomas (former Captain of R.29) was engaged to a young lady from Hull. Those who could afford it found accommodation in Hull or in one of the pleasant villages beside the Humber, from which they could easily commute by car or by one of the two railways serving Howden.

The same two railways gave easy access to the delights of the picture palaces and theatres of Hull and York, which abounded at this time. Musical comedy was in vogue, and revue, and music hall; so that in an average week there was a choice of four or five such confections in the theatres of either city. *The Arcadians* was on tour again and the wartime comedy *The Better 'Ole* (based on cartoonist Bruce Bairnsfather's military caricatures) was being successfully revived at Hull's Alexandria Theatre. One wonders what the US Navy made of Old Bill!

In the dozens of cinema houses, the choices of the time included Charlie Chaplin in *The Kid*; Mary Pickford in *Polyanna* and *Little Lord*

Fauntleroy. Rudolph Valentino as *The Sheik* reflected a new mood of escapism from the realities of postwar depression - to which Tin Pan Alley added *The Sheik of Araby* and other exotic offerings in song.

For those Americans who enjoyed the traditional comforts of the English pub (in spite of warm beer) their pleasure was heightened by the thought that Prohibition had been in force back home since January 1920 in all states except Connecticut and Rhode Island.

As the months passed and the reality of an English winter outweighed some of the pleasures, the inevitable homesickness of servicemen overseas crept in. The delay in getting hands on their airship and the restrictions on flying training, following the loss of R.34, began to rankle. By the time that R.38 - now wearing US Naval colours and the designation ZR-2 - reached Howden in June 1921, most of the American servicemen were eager to depart. The British Air Ministry was also under pressure to complete the contract and to trim down the Airship Service, particularly by closing the huge Howden base which was the size of a small town with all services - gas, water, sewage, electricity, railway and road network - plus enormous hydrogen gas plant.

This mutual impatience was to have tragic consequences.

X

A Difficult Delivery

When the United States Secretary for the Navy approved the purchase of the latest British rigid airship on 9 August 1919 for $2,000,000 he could not have been very sure what he was paying for, considering that Constructor Commander Campbell and his team were still in the process of designing it. All the US Navy had to go on was the specification and the belief that the Limeys knew what they were about. It was like ordering a suit in the latest fashion from the catalogue of a supposedly reputable tailor, with options only in the colour and type of buttons. By way of 'fitting', the US Naval crew was to be given training in Britain, to include flight trials in the new ship. They had to hope (when it was too late to withdraw) that the recent and impending takeover bids - of Shorts by the Admiralty; of the Royal Airship Works by the Air Ministry; of airships by the Royal Air Force - would not affect the quality.

By the time that the Air Ministry took over the RAW on 22 October 1919 only two of the 15 main frames of R.38 had been erected, and it was not until November 1920 that the skeleton neared completion. There was still much to be done in design and modification as well as assembly; and it was inevitable that difficulties unseen on the drawing board would dictate compromises in practice.

Although influenced by the samples dredged up from Zeppelin L.70 and by the interrogation of German prisoners held in France by the talented Flight Lieutenant Pritchard, the designers of R.38 did not intend to build a copy-cat ship.

Everything in the design was worked out from first principles, even to the extent of calculating rather than measuring the weights of standard components such as rivets and girder plates. On paper, R.38 was state of the designers' art in 1920. In the Public Records Office there is a workbook used by Mr C. N. Jacques of the design staff. In it he has tabulated the balancing moments of each component over the entire 699 feet of the hull. As modifications have been introduced, he has reworked the daunting sums, disposing crew members to different stations to restore static balance. Such dedication was typical of the airship designers, but perhaps overloaded with detail, they failed to foresee - or to ascertain - the possibly magnitude of aerodynamic forces in flight. R.38 was to contribute much to the understanding of these forces during her short life.

Meanwhile the on-site foundry and rolling mills turned out the miles of duralumin channels and angle sections and the sheet metal workers stamped out the hundreds of thousands of standard bracing plates - to be assembled like enormous Meccano into girders which in turn became parts for transverse rings or longitudinals. It was repetitive labour-intensive work, requiring much factory floor space; though this stage was dwarfed by the final assembly in the airship shed. Here, on the 700 by 180 feet floor, a pair of $85^1/_2$ feet diameter rings were joined to form the first cylindrical slice of the hull. With one main ring on the trestles and another suspended from the roof, the longitudinals and intermediate rings were inserted and braced to form a complete lattice-work section, which was then hoisted, turned and aligned longitudinally as one bay of the hull framework. Over the months, by this ant-like, spider-like activity, the men and women of the Royal Airship Works spun the intricate, 699 feet long, web of duralumin and steel.

In another part of the sheet metal shop the petrol tanks and more sophisticated shapes were fashioned under the exacting supervision of Mr Owen K. Dawson, Foreman. Dawson exemplifies the type of craftsman available to the engineering industry in the early years of the century, when much still depended on manual skills and professional judgement, and machines were operated by men and not computers. Born at Shipley, Yorkshire in 1889, Dawson served a three-year apprenticeship at the Shipley Metal Working Company before moving through a series of jobs, on promotion, to foreman at the Igranic Electric Company at Bedford in 1914. Exempted from conscription by his skill, he was recruited to Short Brothers' new airship works at Cardington, where even the wooden-framed airships needed to be joined by metal plates and petrol tanks and engine components were of copper and aluminium. With the switch to duralumin construction he held a key position in the process and must have taken great pride in fabricating the world's largest airship. Sadly, his skill could not compensate for flawed design. He was to repeat this experience when he returned to Cardington for the building of the R.101, to see again the wasting of his proud craftsmanship.

* * *

There is a portion of the intestines of cattle known as the *caecum* which has long been used to protect gold leaf during the beating process. It is also impervious to gas, and was for many years the best material to line the gas cells of balloons and airships. As each piece of goldbeaters' skin measured about 40 by 10 inches, it required the sacrifice of up to a million oxen in the Chicago slaughterhouses to serve one airship. The Americans being dedicated carnivores, there was no problem of supply; but the processing was so tedious and messy that it was entrusted to women, who seem better able than men to tolerate such things.

The raw skins were washed and scraped to remove the fat before being soaked in glycerine. They were then glued by rubber solution to cotton panels laid on tables. The panels were stitched into the shape of huge cheeses which were first inflated with air to be checked for leaks from the inside. Deflated and rolled, they were hoisted into the bays of the airship and fitted with the automatic and manoeuvring valves. The first inflation would be carefully watched to ease the bag into its netting without snagging. With the bags gas-filled it became necessary to fasten the hull down to trays of weights, while retaining the slings to the roof of the shed for stability as construction proceeded.

* * *

In the fabric shop, the immense task of tailoring the outer garment for the R.38 consumed many bolts of best linen canvas. The huge silver-doped panels were hoisted into position and laced to the framework, the gaps between sections being sealed by glued canvas strips. The riggers balanced on fire escape ladders or dangled spider-like on bosuns' chairs - a perch neither bigger nor steadier than a child's swing. Very little weight could be put on the delicate girders of the hull, except at joints or along the keel.

The control car and the engine gondolas, which had been assembled separately, were wheeled into place and attached to main-frame joints by struts and bracing wires. Now the work of threading the miles of cables - both manual and electrical - could begin, mostly centralised at the control car but with provision for local emergency operation of ballast and flight controls. Gas and water mains were disposed along the keel; also a system of oil and petrol pipes between the widely distributed tanks.

Engine telegraphs similar to those in a ship were installed in the six power cars, each of which would carry a duty engineer in flight.

In the control car the manual wires were brought to the wheels for rudders and elevators, the release toggles for the ballast bags, the

Fig. 34 R.34, which made the first double Atlantic crossing in 1919, was to have given flight training to the USN crew, but it was wrecked at Howden in a storm following a collision with the North York Moors.

Fig. 35 A North Sea class blimp was used for preliminary flight training.

Fig. 36 R.32, a wooden-framed rigid dirigible copied from the Schütte-Lanz design, on which ZR-2's crew did much of their training after the loss of R.34.

Fig. 37 R.80 - designed by Barnes Wallis at Vickers. Used for training USN airshipmen at Howden.

Fig. 38 Men and women working together on a main ring frame for the airship R.38/ZR-2.

Fig. 39 Hull framing almost complete. The abandoned R.37 is on the left.

Fig. 40 Preparing goldbeater's skin (the caecum of cattle) for lining the gas cells. A big rigid airship would require more than a million skins.

Fig. 41 The skins are stuck to cotton panels and assembled into the cheese-shaped cells. In the background a completed bag is inflated with air to test for leaks.

gas manoeuvring valves, and the master engine telegraph *annunciator*. Telephones served the remoter parts of the ship, backed by voice pipes to key crew stations. Communication with the ground or surface vessels could be by Aldis lamp or a powerful Dean horn, both keying the Morse code. For more distant contact there was the cumbersome wireless telegraphy equipment in its cabin abaft the navigating room.

The more conventional navigation instruments of compass, altimeter and airspeed indicator were supplemented by some which were essential to airship flying. They included *barometer, inclinometer* and *rise and fall indicator*; also the crucial thermometers and pressure gauges from which the lifting power of the gas was calculated and changes anticipated.

The highly specialised work of instrumentation and electrical layout was under the resident eye of Flight Lieutenant A. J. Osborn, RAF, representing the Deputy Director of Research (Instruments).

All the work of fabrication and inspection came under Mr Stephen Payne, who was also deputy to Constructor-Commander Campbell although with no responsibility for design. Officially he headed the separate Construction and Inspection Departments, and had to answer for the shed, workshops, foundry, rolling mill, fabric shop and gas plant. The exclusion of the Design Section (and presumably the Drawing Office) from his empire may not have been a problem in practice, but it did create an odd administrative situation when he was acting as Deputy Manager during Campbell's frequent absences, as presumably he could not answer for design decisions.

From the inception of the planning of the Admiralty 'A' Class dirigibles, Mr Henry May had carried an increasing load of responsibility as assistant to C. I. R. Campbell. May was a Royal Naval Constructor who had transferred to airships in 1917 and had been part of the team which had designed the successful R.33 and R.34 (based on the *Little Wigborough* Zeppelin L.33). Although not officially Campbell's deputy - this post being held by Stephen Payne - May had watched over the assembly of R.38 from the beginning and was familiar with every detail. It was he who supervised the inflation of the gas cells and advised the new Head of Design Mr H. B. Wynn Evans - an ex-Barrow RCNC designer of submarines who had been transferred to airship work. Evans had just returned from Germany, no doubt inspired by his examination of the surviving Zeppelins, and most likely comfortable in the knowledge that R.38's *basic* design was someone else's work. During Campbell's frequent absences at meetings, conferences and lectures, May carried much of the responsibility and consequent worry about the *overall* soundness of the design, and had to ensure that any significant new work and modifications would be compatible with the original conception. We shall never know whether he was aided or undermined in this task by the shadowy figure of Mr Uren, who was an inspector of design features reporting *directly* to Campbell, independently of the Inspection Department.

For the supervision of construction there was a competent team of foremen and inspectors to ensure that everything was according to the detail drawings supplied by the former Short Brother's drawing office. For example there was Mr Albert Edward Gerrish, Shed and Shops Manager, who as an ex-Beardmore (Inchinnan) overseer had helped to build R.34. It was he who saw that the drawings were translated into actual hardware, and who also initiated repairs of defects and carried out modifications requested by the design staff. It was in the matter of these minor changes that Campbell asserted himself in January 1921, when it was revealed that section leaders and the drawing office were 'saving time' by making such decisions on the shop floor. A stern memo set up a system for registering all changes to drawings with the Curator, who held a set of master plans and all amendments.

Constantly on Gerrish's heels and alert for flaws or deviations from specification was Mr H. McWade of the Aeronautical Inspection Directorate (AID) who would ultimately have to pronounce R.38 fit for work, even though, as a *service* ship, she did not require a Certificate of Airworthiness. He must have been a worried man when his assistant Mr Jenkins accidentally discovered R.38's Achilles heel while checking bracing wire tensions. It happened that some damage was caused to the top of Frame 8 during the first test inflation of No.8 gas bag. After repairs and minor modifications the bag was reinflated and Jenkins was again dangled from the roof to check the tensions in the radial and chord bracing wires. In order to reach two of the wires he hauled himself along a girder which promptly buckled under the extra *compressive* and *lateral* loads which he thus imposed, causing a number of others to collapse due to the resulting imbalance. Presumably in the knowledge that Mr Jenkins would not dangle during the flight and that the top of the ship was normally in *tension* due to the hogging weight of the bow mooring gear and the compensatory ballast aft, the damaged girders were replaced with slight reinforcement at the joints. That many of the *lower* girders of the hull could experience varying degrees of *compression* does not seem to have worried anyone at this stage, as it was assumed that the substantial keel corridor would act as a backbone. Perhaps if Campbell had watched a dog wagging its tail he might have realised that *lateral* flexing, such as would occur during turning, invariably compresses each flank alternately to a greater extent than the spine.

*   *   *

Fig. 42 Key construction staff at Cardington in front of the control car which
reminded witness Charles Ayre of an electric tram.
Seated: L. Burman, A. Beattie, C. Quantrell, Barrett.
Standing: G. Cook, W. Bligh, O.K. Dawson, Unknown.

Fig. 43 The control car - showing helm (centre), elevator wheel and engine telegraphs
(right).

Fig. 44 R.38 becomes ZR-2

Fig. 45 Achilles Heel: The collapse of girders on Transverse Frame 8 during the test inflation of Gas Cell 8.

From the arrival of the United States contingent at Howden in April 1920, their interests at Cardington were served by the looming presence of Commander Horace T. Dyer, USN. Impressively tall, he dominates the contemporary group photographs taken with the RAW hierarchy and visiting US Naval airshipmen. As the man on the spot, he not only kept an eye on quality but also had to negotiate with the Air Ministry for the modifications required by the US Navy. These included the bow gear for mast mooring, positions for fourteen machine guns and racks for twelve bombs (4 of 520 lb and 8 of 230 lb). The bombs were to be carried nose-uppermost for ease of fusing in flight. Additional gravity petrol tanks were requested over each engine car for quick starting - a prudent provision when the main fuel supply was distributed along the frames in fifty separate tanks of 190 gallons each. As some of these changes were requested quite late in the building programme (already running behind time) he needed to be something of a diplomat.

From time to time Dyer was joined by C. P. Burgess, an American airship constructor who had the unenviable job of checking the strength calculations for R.38. He found this a daunting and confusing task because the calculations filled thirty separate work books and included tentative calculations which led nowhere. However, he formed the opinion as early as July 1920 that the Admiralty method of calculating stresses in main frames was likely to lead to large errors. He was later critical of the fact that only *static* forces had been considered in the design, but he paid tribute to the courage of the designers who had to work with the limited knowledge of the time.

Another source of irritation to the Americans was the reluctance of the Air Ministry to allow US Naval observers to fly with the British rigids still in service, except in the designated training ships R.32 and R.80. After some argument, a few key officers and CPOs were taken as passengers on R.33's exercises, but the general shortage of flying time for the Howden Detachment remained a sore point. Most of all, they were becoming impatient to get their hands on their own ship.

The time factor was also worrying others, though in different ways. For the RAW management teams there was the Air Ministry's insistence on haste during the critical final stages of construction and inspection - always an engineer's nightmare. It is in such situations that details may be overlooked, and the legend of the missing cottar pin may become a reality. To compound the problems, the workforce, which had so far not expedited its own redundancy, was offered overtime and a bonus for completion by 7 June. Such inducements are not compatible with dedicated craftsmanship and this in turn put an added strain on the inspectors. As late as March 1921, Campbell had been alerted to apparent weakness in the rudder and elevator pintles, and these had to be quickly remade. Many other details required attention after the bonus had been collected, and it was not until 23 June that the huge fledgling was very gently eased from her nest into the calm evening air for her first tentative flight.

XI

Trials - and Tribulations

As R.38/ZR-2 approached the end of her incubation, some increasingly worried men were devising the test schedule which would culminate in the proving flights and acceptance by the United States Navy. There was also the need for a familiarisation programme for the USN crew who would deliver the ZR-2 to her home base at Lakehurst, New Jersey, where a gigantic shed, 'the largest and most perfectly equipped building of its kind in the world' was being constructed at a cost of $2,000,000. It measured 912 feet (278m) by 279 feet (85m) and was 193 feet (59m) high. It could accommodate two airships of ZR-2 size. Not scheduled for completion until late 1921, it had been a good reason for not rushing the construction of ZR-2 during the early stages. Following the delays back at Cardington, this time of grace was running out, and both British and American interests were pressing for an early delivery. Commander Maxfield, captain-designate, was insistent that the trans-Atlantic flight should be not later than the end of August. This suited the Air Ministry, increasingly eager to be relieved of airships, but was hardly prudent for a new ship of unproven performance.

The Royal Air Force officer designated to oversee the trials was the highly qualified and respected Major Pritchard, OBE, AFC, whose American profile was suitably high by virtue of dual nationality (from his father) and his spectacular parachute landing from R.34 in 1919. On 21 February 1921 he was officially loaned as Senior Assistant to the Director General of Supply and Research with the new RAF rank of Flight Lieutenant. With his wide experience of airship flying embracing SS, Coastal, Parseval and Rigid types, and an exceptional technical background including his study of Zeppelins, he was the obvious choice to plan the test programme. His planning was to be thwarted by men of lesser talent but superior rank.

To allow for the proving of new features and likely modifications in what was essentially an *experimental* ship, Pritchard specified a progressive working up to culminate in a substantial flight in rough weather conditions. Only then should the comparatively green USN crew take delivery for their familiarisation flights. He devised a serial programme of 150 hours. Maxfield disagreed, and on 6 June he and some of his colleagues met Air Ministry officers to propose a modified and much curtailed programme, demanding that the RAF tests should be completed in *one* day, after which ZR-2 would complete 12-hour and 24-hour flights with the American crews, but with RAF Flight Lieutenants Wann and Little as in-flight advisers. As justification, he said that he 'did not want more than 50 hours put on the ship' before he took over. Even some of his own officers felt that this was pushing their luck, but it pleased the Air Ministry, and it was provisionally agreed that 50 hours would suffice; with the *British* tests ideally compressed into the first flight.

As ADC Howden, General (now Air Commodore) Edward Maitland was in charge of Rigid Airship testing and was therefore ultimately responsible for the proving flights of R.38. He was appalled by this decision and immediately protested, to be told somewhat rudely not to give advice unless he was asked for it, and to hand over the ship to the US Navy as soon as the Director General of Supply and Research had passed her as fit.

Pritchard was now in an impossible position. As the DGSR's Senior Assistant he was instructed to pronounce the ship airworthy, but within 50 flying hours. This meant that the gently escalating trials would have to be compressed by combining several tests in each flight. It inevitably meant pushing the new ship to the limit. In addition, as a professional engineer, he was eager to allow the dedicated Mr Pannell of the NPL to complete his wind tunnel calibration tests. More than anyone, with the possible exception of Maitland, these two dedicated and intelligent men would have appreciated the risks they were taking.

There was another problem for Pritchard, who was fully aware of the *height climbing* ancestry of the R.38/ZR-2 design. He had, after all, been the officer who had examined the grounded Zeppelins and interrogated their crews in France, reporting his findings to C. I. R. Campbell in February 1918. He had also represented the Admiralty's airship interests on the Inter-Allied Armistice Commission in 1918 and at the Peace Conference in Paris in 1919, for which he had been awarded the OBE. He was well aware that height-climbing Zeppelins did not attempt violent use of controls below 7,500 feet, at which height the loads on control surfaces would be about half of the forces at around 2,000 feet; but to ascend to that height would involve the automatic valving of hydrogen - which would have to be replenished before the next flight, with consequent delay. Also, the truncated programme ruled out rough weather flying, for a very simple reason. No mooring mast existed at Cardington in 1921, which decreed that each flight began and ended with the tricky journey from the shed, where there was very little clearance at the doors. Successful docking was only likely to happen if a flat calm could be predicted over the entire flight period. The rarity of flat calms, except at dawn and dusk, and the need to avoid superheating and consequent loss of gas virtually compelled a night flight from Cardington. There was a mast at Pulham - but Pulham did not have the range of workshops which might be required for repairs and modifications during the tests. So it had been decided that the initial tests should be conducted from Cardington with the final acceptance trials based on Howden, which had no mast but a large shed. Only then would *United States Airship ZR-2* be moored to the Pulham mast. It followed that the only possible approximation to rough weather conditions would be by stressful manoeuvring in the dense air at low level.

Thus was the issue decided - in ignorance by the non-airship officials at the Air Ministry and by the informed courage of officers who were unwilling to release a ship of *unproven* strength.

* * *

The eagerly awaited emergence of R.38 from the Cardington shed on 23 June was accomplished without ruffling her feathers, in itself a considerable feat of organisation and discipline by hundreds of workers and servicemen who walked her out. To the gentlemen of the press and the spectators (the latter barred from the airfield) she was a thing of undoubted beauty and majesty, and the very last word in aviation at 9 o'clock on that warm summer evening. Fifty-two minutes later she lifted off gently for a first seven hour flight; a considerable act of faith in view of the number of design innovations and an occurrence in the shed earlier in the day. During the *weighing off,* some of her gas cells had been overfilled while the designers were at lunch. A sudden rise in temperature had expanded the hydrogen more quickly than the automatic valves could release it and the overfed bags had popped a number of circumferential steel tapes which had replaced the conventional hemp netting used in previous rigids. Later there was to be speculation that the tapes had been brittle due to age and to the neglect of anti-corrosive varnishing until after assembly; but for the present the initial flight could proceed with caution. A subsequent slackening of the corset-like tapes was deemed to be all that was necessary for her comfort.

* * *

The honour and responsibility of taking two and three quarter million cubic feet of untried dirigible into the sky had fallen to Flight Lieutenant Archibald Wann, an airship pilot of experience and known skill. Originally in the Royal Navy, he had volunteered 'for special purposes' (the euphemism for airship training) at the end of 1915. He had experience of anti-submarine work and had been to Russia as British airship representative - a somewhat thankless task considering that the blimps sent to Russia, like a number of Spitfires and Hurricanes of a later war, were never even unpacked. After the war he conducted the first trial of R.36, which was a 'stretched' copy of Zeppelin L.48 (shot down at Theberton, Suffolk on 17 June 1917). He was well known to the Howden Detachment, whose training he had supervised on R.32 and R.80.

For First Officer he had the services of Flight Lieutenant I. C. Little, AFC, a former captain of R.32 and several earlier ships. The navigator was Flight Lieutenant R. S. Montagu, DSC, and Flying Officer T. F. Matthewson, AFC, was engineer officer.

This experienced group, under the *direction* but not *command* of Flight Lieutenant Pritchard, had the doubtful pleasure of the company of Air Commodore Sir Robert Brooke-Popham, CB, CMG, DSO, AFC. As Director-General of Supply and Research at the Air Ministry he outranked everyone involved with R.38, including Maitland, who was Director of Airships as well as AOC Howden. Brooke-Popham had a distinguished war career, but his experience was confined to aeroplanes. In lighter-than-air matters he was advised by Wing Commander T. R. Cave-Brown-Cave, that talented airship engineer who had been one of the innovators of the Submarine Scout in 1915, and who with Pritchard had designed the *Parasuit*.

Regardless of whether the crew and passengers could afford the Parasuit or elected to wear the humbler home-made canvas harness, there were parachutes for all; of the clip-on, static-line-operated pattern. Individually allocated by Sgt. Mason, they were checked, packed and installed at crew stations by the dedicated AC.1 'Brainy' Dobbs. Himself a veteran of 59 drops, his presence on the first three trials may have demonstrated confidence in his parachutes if not in the ship.

Not surprisingly, the distinguished passenger list included Edward Maitland and C. I. R. Campbell; and as the result of some wrangling with the Air Ministry, Commander Maxfield, Lieutenant Commander Bieg and two senior ratings representing the US Navy.

Now, at 9.52 am on the 23 June 1921, Wann signalled *hands off* to the ground crew, telegraphed the engine cars for *slow ahead* and gently eased R.38 to her *pressure height* of 2,300 feet - the height at which the gas cells were dilated. A further rise to 2,500 feet provided a controlled test of the automatic valves (under suspicion following their earlier tardiness) which would also equalise the percentage fullness of each bag and thus the pressure in adjacent cells during any sudden rise. As the earlier gas bag tests had shown, unequal pressures could cause serious damage. Height was then decreased to 1,800 feet for manoeuvring trials.

At first all went well, but as speed was increased to 38 knots (45mph) the coxswains reported difficulty in moving their wheels, to the extent of causing the cycle-type chain connections to the control cables to slip over their sprockets. This put both elevator and rudder pairs out of step and thwarted any notion of completing the trials in one flight. Examination showed that the long control cables had stretched, allowing the slack sides to wrap themselves round the taut sides and so jam the movement. Prudently waiting for daybreak, Wann landed his warp-winged fledgling at Cardington, where the weary handlers returned it to its nest at 5am.

In spite of the lack of positive results from the first flight, Pritchard and Wann felt that the experimental rudders and elevators had been over-balanced by placing too much area in front of the pivots; so it was decided, against the marked reluctance of Commander Campbell, to make an arbitrary reduction of the balancing horn of the top rudder. A tentative 9 inch strip was taken off the leading edge.

To overcome the jamming problem strong springs were coupled into the control wires to take up any slack. Some minor modifications were also carried out, including the replacement of the bottom transverse girder at Frame 13 and the connecting longitudinals to Frame 14. These had been distorted by a static fin test before the first flight, possibly assisted by crewmen's boots - the G-G longitudinals being the supports for the walkway where it entered the fin.

* * *

On the night of 28/29 June a second flight of six hours was made with the prime purpose of settling the control balancing argument. Wann was again in command, with Pritchard supervising tests agreed between the designers and NPL representatives Pannell and Frazer. To decide whether the cropping of the upper rudder had improved the balance, the lower rudder was disengaged and then locked centrally by clamping its cables together. Various helm angles were tried at increasing speeds, with results which at first sight seemed inconsistent, as large rudder movements were easily corrected until the final few degrees whenever 5° either side of centre caused problems. Further tests were made with the bottom rudder clamped off-centre. It was deduced that the swing of the ship's tail while turning had a considerable effect on the balancing; but with time pressing, and having discussed the problem with the officers who had been on the flight, it was surmised that the control planes *were* generally overbalanced, whatever else might be amiss.

Back in the Cardington shed there was some dramatic surgery. A further 14 inches was trimmed from the top rudder, 23 inches from each elevator horn and 18 inches from the lower rudder. 'A certain amount' was also trimmed off the trailing edges of the top rudder and elevators, reducing the area of the central surfaces by about 10% in total. The helm ratio was also increased from $5^1/_2$ turns to 8 turns of the wheel for complete reversal of the rudder, a modification prompted by Zeppelin practice of low gearing to ensure gentle application of controls.

With time and the buyers' patience running out, the 'final' modifications were put in hand, including the resiting of the service petrol tanks from the cars to the hull, as requested by the Americans. Other alterations carried out at this time suggest that weaknesses had been observed at various points during the first two flights; for example, double bracing was applied to the frames supporting the 2,000lb. water ballast bags. Another significant measure was the dispersal of food lockers and water tanks 'to avoid concentration of weight in Crew Space'. Further evidence that this was cause for concern is given by the unsigned loading instructions 'issued some date prior to 25th July to C. O. Ship and to Comdr. Maxfield on 17th August 1921', according to the handwritten annotation on the Court of Inquiry's copy. It is a typewritten sheet of eighteen items, none of which relates to balancing or flying the airship; rather it is a list of *don'ts* about *concentrations* of weights within the delicate framework. Five of the prohibitions relate to bodies, notably that

> '*not more than 15 persons should be allowed in the crew space at any time and not more than 2 persons should be allowed on any five metre length of the corridor walking way girder at the same time*' [Author's italics, but the entire document, which is given in Fig. 88 of this book, is worthy of emphasis.]

Considering the average sailor's or airman's attitude to regulations, it could have taken a sizeable staff of ship's police to enforce these rules in a vessel of such size and complexity.

* * *

Fig. 46 One of the elevators, showing the heavy dynamic balancing area which had
to be reduced after control problems in flight.
The tail cockpit is just visible to the right of the large pulley block.

Fig. 47 R.38/ZR-2 emerges from the Cardington shed for the first time on 23 June
1921. (Shed No.2 was not transferred from Pulham until 1928.)

Fig. 48 R.38/ZR-2 leaves Cardington for Howden on 17 July 1921. Its next flight was its fourth and last.

Fig. 49 Howden at last. R.38 - now ZR-2 - in the huge double shed.

The time had now come for what should have been the acceptance of R.38 by the Air Ministry, prior to handing it to its new owners as ZR-2. Because of the telescoping of the test programme there seems to have been an overlap of the formalities as well, and as a Certificate of Airworthiness was not required for a service ship, it is not clear to what extent the inspection by Mr McWade of the AID was either complete, wholehearted or merely provisional. [This honourable man was to face the same dilemma nine years later over the certification of R.101.] Authorisation of each flight seems to have been in the form of telegrams and/or letters between Cardington and Air Commodore Brooke-Popham at the Air Ministry. The reality was that when R.38 left her builders to fly to Howden for her official but largely notional AM acceptance trials, she had yet to prove that the modified controls would work. Strictly speaking, this was a *design* matter and therefore still the responsibility of the Royal Airship Works.

Discounting the financial and political bodies on both sides of the Atlantic - as ever keeping their distance from actual consequences of their actions - it is interesting to note the number of fingers in the pie at this stage, viz.,

Royal Airship Works - designers and builders.
Royal Air Force - trials crew and officers seconded to
    RAW and AM.
Air Ministry - (a) Director General of Supply and Research.
              (b) Aeronautical Inspection Department.
National Physical Laboratory - fin pressure tests and
    wind tunnel calibration.
United States Navy - observers and potential customer.

Representatives in human form of all these interests were involved at each stage of testing; but though working to a common end their professional and personal requirements were conflicting.

Campbell, with his reputation as a designer on the line, had the added burden of the safety of the ship to consider, and he must have been torn between wanting the most stringent testing but with a more prudent escalation of the risk.

Pritchard was concerned that the ship might survive its acceptance trials only to meet its doom in the rough Atlantic weather.

McWade's duty was not only to ensure that the ship had been built faithfully to the drawings, but also to detect any signs of structural unsoundness - but how could that be honestly and fully determined without flying it?

Pannell and his NPL colleagues had their best test vehicle to date in R.38, but for a very limited time, and their long-term aims were only incidental to the immediate trials programme.

Brooke-Popham had to reconcile the strongly expressed warnings of his experts with the impatience of his political and financial masters.

In the American camp, opinions were divided between eager fliers, pressing for delivery, and the cautious and professional engineer Commander Dyer and his associates. At least some of their misgivings seem to have worried responsible people at home and at the US Embassy in London, where Ambassador Harvey had even considered asking the Navy Department to cancel the purchase. Confiding in his military attaches and some friends during the fourth and last flight he said,

> I distrust the whole undertaking of the R.38 crossing the Atlantic, particularly at this time. . . . When I saw the airship at Pulham [sic] . . . I had an involuntary distrust of the whole business, and have really worried a great deal about it.

At least one CPO of the Howden Detachment shared his misgivings, but at a more personal level. In a letter to colleagues at Rockaway Air Station N.Y., he referred to the 'screwy' controls of the 'lousy lemon'.

* * *

With so much still unresolved, R.38 left Cardington for the last time in the calm evening air of 17 July for Howden and her metamorphosis into ZR-2. She left behind a sense of anticlimax and insecurity among the RAW staff. Lipscomb and the retained Short Brothers draughtsmen posed for a farewell photograph and prepared for a move to Rochester, probably not yet aware that their experience with light alloy design would be invaluable for aircraft building within a very short time.

Waiting for R.38/ZR-2, with the unenviable task of resolving the conflicting demands, was the highly respected General (now Air Commodore) Edward Maitland, CMG, DSO, AFC, Air Officer Commanding Howden. As Director of Airships, his was the ultimate responsibility of pronouncing the ship airworthy. A dedicated airman, he was also aware that the future, if any, of British lighter-than-air flight depended on the performance of *US Naval Airship ZR-2.* Any subsequent defects, whether structural or operational, could ruin Britain's credibility as airship builders. It would be a double folly to hand over an untried ship to an untrained crew - but that was exactly what he was being urged to do.

As R.38 droned through the darkness towards Howden, the modified controls were again tested at increasing speeds and angles.

Up to 45 knots (51³/₄ mph) there was a marked improvement in handling, with no straining by the coxswains. Wann felt confident enough to put some Americans on the helm and elevators and to hand over command to Ivor Little, the First Officer. Shortly before midnight, Mr Pannell of the NPL requested an increase of speed to 50 knots (57¹/₂ mph) in pursuance of his fin and rudder tests. Pritchard, who had remained on duty, objected that at under 2,500 feet there was insufficient margin for error in the event of a control failure; and that furthermore the percentage volume in the bags should first be equalised at pressure height to avoid any damage in the event of a sudden rise if the elevators should jam. Little was adamant; Wann had told him not to exceed pressure height, which was about 2,300 feet at that time, and in his own opinion there was no danger.

The forward and rear pairs of engines were now opened up and a confident Commander Maxfield and apprehensive Flight Lieutenant Pritchard watched the airspeed increase to 50 knots and the altitude rise to 2,200 feet. One of the few experienced American coxswains, CMM James 'Red' Collier, had the elevator control, having just relieved CBM Charles Aller. Suddenly the controls became 'somewhat awkward to handle', in Pritchard's understated later report, and the ship dived 500 feet before being forced into a sharp climb by Pritchard, who had unceremoniously seized the wheel from Collier. With some difficulty he coaxed the skittish ship back to almost level flight, although it still 'hunted' by 100 feet about a mean altitude.

Almost at once the intercom telephone rang in the control car. It was a shaken Charlie Aller, reporting that girders had buckled at frame 7 as he was returning aft to the crew space. Little immediately rang for reduced revs and the hunting motion settled down. It was obvious that the controls were still overbalanced at higher speeds and that the USN helmsman had been caught unawares by the elevators toppling.

Examination with flashlights showed that an intermediate transverse and a longitudinal girder were badly damaged; so on two engines and reduced revs a course was set for landing at Howden at first light after about nine hours in the air. A detailed inspection, with the ship securely tethered to the roof and floor of the shed, revealed that in addition to broken girders on the port side a number of adjacent members had been strained, supposedly by 'propeller wash' (slipstream) in the opinion of C. I. R. Campbell, although Stephen Payne suspected resonance of the girders with the period of vibration of the propeller. The fact that the midships engines - attached to the hull at Frame 7 - were *idling* at the time of breakage does not seem to have been taken into account.

During the following weeks, in the huge Double Rigid Shed at Howden, the failed and suspect girders were cut out and replaced by staff sent from Cardington. This included all the lower keel main and intermediate longitudinals (i.e. the F and F' girders) between Frames 7 and 8 aft of the midships engine car attachments. Additionally it was decided to stiffen all intermediate transverse girders between the F and G longitudinals from Frames 5 to 10 - almost a third of the airship's length - by riveting on reverse channels. This rule of thumb modification was defended by Stephen Payne at the subsequent inquiry:

> All these were not broken or bent, but it was considered desirable to stiffen beyond where weakness actually occurred.

By now the conscientious and knowledgeable John Pritchard had grave doubts about the basic design and he submitted several reports to Air Commodore Maitland on the tests to date, stressing that the ship was far from being proven fit to face

> the increasingly bad weather in the Atlantic and on the American coast which is likely to be encountered after the end of August.

No tests had yet been conducted in disturbed air conditions,

> and therefore, from the airworthiness and staunchness point of view, the trials so far carried out are of little value. It is necessary that before the ship flies to America she should first be proved to be airworthy by British personnel and then be handed over to the Americans who will carry out one or two flights in her to accustom themselves to her general behaviour.

To underline his concern he pointed out that great liberties had been taken with factors of safety in the pursuit of maximum performance, and recommended that further tests should be in accordance with Zeppelin *height climber* practice of strenuous control movements *only above 7,000 feet*, with correspondingly gentle manoeuvres in the dense lower air. While this would not prove her *staunchness* it might satisfy the *airworthiness* criteria, and she might live to be tested in rough air at a later date. As for the theory that hard usage at lower altitude would simulate turbulent air stresses, this still remained to be proved by research and practice - but only after she had shown good flying behaviour.

Ironically, he had ample time to write because a period of disturbed weather had prevented the tricky operation of removing the ship - now irrevocably designated ZR-2 in large letters - from the shed for testing in the rough air which was now available. In his capacity as the Air Ministry representative he also wrote to his boss, the Director General of Supply and Research. Unfortunately Air Commodore Sir Robert Brooke-Popham, CB, CMG, DSO, AFC, was in Egypt, but in his name a minute to the Chief of Air Staff (the intimidating and anti-airship Air Vice Marshall Sir Hugh 'Boom' Trenchard) certified on 2 August that R.38/ZR-2 was ready for delivery. By a stroke of the pen, in the absence of the one man with authority to extend the trials, the ship and many good men were condemned to death. Execution was not to be long delayed.

The repairs and modifications having been completed by 30 July, and with Commander Maxfield determined to move to the Pulham mooring mast for final preparations by mid-August, there could be no reprieve - only a short stay of execution due to the unfavourable weather.

XII

Expectations and Frustrations

In the impoverished Britain of the 1920s the airship was high on the list of endangered species, competing for very scarce resources in a country beggared by four years of the most wasteful war in history. Even its more ploughshare-like advantages in terms of endurance and reliability had been challenged by the Atlantic crossing of Alcock and Brown in a mere *aeroplane*, not to mention the dogged (if partial) success by the United States Navy's NC flying boat team. There was the probability that the cheaper and less demanding aeroplane might yet be developed as the long-range carrier of passengers and goods, in addition to its proven military uses.

Understandably, a number of wartime aviators had left the RAF in search of safer work and a settled career, leaving a nucleus of enthusiasts and professionals to carry on with the resources available. The impending demise of the airship service did not invalidate the expertise of its members, who would automatically transfer to heavier-than-air operations; taking with them a knowledge of navigation, meteorology, engineering and radio in excess of anything possessed *at that time* by most aeroplane personnel. With global travel at last a possibility there was a lot to be learned from those who had 'been there'.

In this context, seldom in the history of aeronautics can so many rare eggs have been placed in one basket as in the final crew list for R.38/ZR-2's fourth trial. The joint RAF, USN and civilian personnel included ten airship pilots, two engineering officers and two radio officers; also the American navigation expert, Lieutenant Commander Richard Byrd, finally in with a chance to fly the Atlantic after his exclusion from the USN flying boat expedition, and the loss of the non-rigid C-5, which he was to have navigated from Newfoundland to England in 1919.

The non-commissioned crew members had been selected from the most experienced coxswains, riggers and engineers available; although to one disappointed RAF sergeant, rejected for an inadequate shave on parade, the selection may have seemed arbitrary. The American other ranks were predominantly regular navy chief petty officers with the motivation of being in an elite service with a bright future.

As for Constructor-Commander Campbell, he was an experienced and innovative engineer with a solid reputation in airship construction; as yet unchallenged by his young Vickers rivals, Pratt and Wallis. Perhaps rather inclined to keep too much in his own busy hands and head and lacking the technical and administrative backup which later became the norm, he was nevertheless poised on the brink of a promising career in aviation, in which aircraft would without doubt get bigger and more complex.

To answer for the new Sunbeam *Cossack* engines, (relatively sinless compared with the airframe problems), Mr Frank Warren was the only other RAW member on the flight list. From the time that the Cossacks had been chosen, he had worked closely with the Sunbeam factory at Wolverhampton and had helped to plan the power car installation.

Also in the basket were three dedicated NPL scientists (Pannell, Duffield, Bateman), with the double task of assessing the forces on the control surfaces and to make sense of the *scale effect* between real aircraft and models in a wind tunnel; the latter to become a major design tool. There was another, more intangible, but equally vulnerable passenger. It was *British Prestige*.

* * *

Waiting at Howden for the fourth flight, which was to combine the final tests and the official USN acceptance trials, imposed a gratuitous strain on personnel who had already endured the tensions and frustrations of the first three flights and the subsequent modifications. Everything possible had been completed, including additional sleeping accommodation and a separate crew space for the officers. Final preparations for the ocean crossing would have to wait until ZR-2 could ride at the Pulham mooring mast, but for almost three weeks a succession of Atlantic depressions had driven a blustery wind across the Yorkshire flatlands to confine ZR-2 to the shed.

Importunate pressmen hung about the big event and justified their expenses by cabling background information about the crewmen and their families, together with any 'scuttlebutt' concerning the new ship's weaknesses. The trained ear of the

Associated Press correspondent homed him in on Lieutenant Marcus H. Esterley, USN, the designated radio officer of ZR-2. The 30 year old Naval Reservist was the butt of some amusement over his provision of a small balloon to carry an emergency radio to 250 feet in the event of a forced landing at sea. He was questioned about the confidence of his colleagues over the Atlantic crossing. Esterley assured him that they were not worried, but that he considered it prudent to prepare for anything which might happen. For its time, it was an advanced idea which foreshadowed the use of dingy radios with kite flown aerials in WWII.

Back home, the United States taxpayers were being primed to receive their expensive purchase by means of press releases which gave details of the crew as well as the ship, naming their home town origins in addition to their ranks and duties. It was a time of upsurge in the national confidence, following their successful participation in the Great War but before the Great Depression was to take it all away. The country was wildly airminded, and people flocked to the barnstorming visits of the air circuses to see daredevil stunts by war surplus aeroplanes and pilots. Those with a wider vision could already visualise the potential of aerial communication in a large country with widely scattered centres of population. Major Charles J. Glidden, President of the *World's Board of Aeronautical Commissioners, Inc.*, was urging a flag-showing tour by ZR-2 to the West Coast, perhaps hoping to impress potential investors in air travel as well as the taxpayer. At Lakehurst, home station for the new Navy dirigible, Captain Frank T. Evans was told to 'hasten the work of completing the hanger, employing the civilian labour on overtime if necessary'.

Possibly to pre-empt any cheeky Limey exhibitionism at the landing - Pritchard would be a passenger on the delivery flight! - the ground handling party were to have some practice with D-6, a non-rigid about the same size as a Coastal.

To mar the public enthusiasm, reports of the girder problems had at last leaked to the press, reluctantly confirmed by the Navy Department but accompanied by a confident statement from Maitland, who was greatly respected on both sides of the Atlantic. He added that he would not permit the departure until the weather was favourable, although it is hard to imagine that he could have influenced the strong-willed Maxfield after the official handover; it was Maxfield who had insisted on the reduction of the trial hours.

Among the inevitable prophets of doom who did not make the headlines, there was a Mr J. W. Cann who claimed to speak from 'extensive practical experience in inventing, designing and construction, also running of petrol engines, motor cars and coaches since 1901'. He claimed to have served three years in the Aeronautical Inspection Department and also some months in tanks.

He was now studying airships and had proposed a suitable design to be known as the *Silkworm*. Armed with a rough sketch of his invention and a letter of introduction to Commander Maxfield, he descended upon Howden on 11 August, where next day he was shown over ZR-2 by Flight Lieutenant Montagu, RAF. Nothing seems to have pleased him, and he was particularly critical of carrying petrol in proximity to the gas bags and to electrical wiring - a legitimate worry which he spoiled by a fanciful theory about how 'leaks from the magneto base . . . would course from the highly charged engine and ignite and rush the petrol tanks . . .'. Dismissing Montagu's explanations about the earthing and bonding of the pipes he said: 'God help your ship. In my opinion it will never reach America'.

Later, and somewhat smugly in view of events, he declared himself to the Air Ministry as 'free and willing to design in detail a suitable airship that would be quite safe and trustworthy'.

* * *

For the Howden Detachment there were the emotions - familiar to generations of servicemen overseas - of 'waiting for the boat'. Farewells had been said, and repeated; kitbags had been searched for clean underwear and socks; living-out personnel had returned to barracks. With a few exceptions the wives of USN personnel, including most of the recently acquired British brides, had already departed by sea, while there were inevitable regrets by local girls who had, in a manner of speaking, missed the boat. In nearby Howden town there was the impending dual loss of income and excitement, as ZR-2's departure heralded the end of the airship station. The crew lists had been posted for the final test flight and for the trans-Atlantic delivery. The lack of meaningful activity added to the air of impatience and uncertainty.

At last on 18 August it seemed that the weather was to stabilise. The crewmen and test specialists were hastily summoned and the three-hundred strong handling party was put on standby. Next day, in obvious frustration, Pritchard scribbled a report headed *4th Trial Flight R.38 - The false alarm*. It gives a graphic picture of the excitement generated by the world's largest flying machine. It is worth quoting an extract. He wrote:

> The most annoying part of airship trials is the very weary waiting for perfect weather. This is only necessary during the trial period and it is most gruelling to sit still . . . while tried-out airships in service are carrying out regular flying. On Thursday

[18 August] the prospects looked most promising . . .
the ship being scheduled to leave as soon as the daily
temperature wind had died down just before sunset.

Disappointment may have given an uncharacteristic sharpness
to his words, or it may have been a symptom of the strain of the
protracted responsibility. He was also missing his wife and three
children at Cherry Tree Corner, Chorley Wood.

Howden Airship Station is usually a dismal flat plain
only a few feet above sea level, but on this occasion it
was a scene of surprising activity, the local aborigines
lined up [sic] the roads surrounding the large landing
ground as the evening approached. Every imaginable
form of conveyance slowly collected, from the homely
donkey-cart to the luxurious high powered limousine.
The patience of these people was truly remarkable, as
was also the speed with which rumour must have
spread the news of a possible flight, for so many
people to collect.

In this last sentence he has underestimated the closeness of a
provincial community and above all the degree of integration
between the airship station and its locality. He was, by frequent
exposure, more used to the press.

The difference between the patient onlookers and the
energetic bustling reporters, press photographers and
camera operators was extreme and the different way
in which each class regarded the flight, the reporters
hungry for every crumb of information as to where
the ship was going to fly to and what she was going to
do. The photographers were hoping . . . that the ship
would go out before the light became too bad to take
good photographs. So far, R.38 on each of her 3
previous trial flights, has been a confirmed night-bird,
leaving after sunset and landing again at dawn, and
the resulting discomfiture of the photographers has
been pathetic.

In the latter context it should be remembered that press
photographers in 1921 were armed with cumbersome cameras using
glass negatives or filmpacks, and that the almost exclusively black-
and-white stock was of slow speed. The magnesium flash equipment
of the time could not illuminate more than a few square yards -

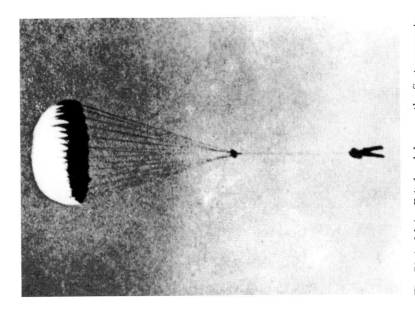

Fig. 51 As Major Pritchard, he was the first person to arrive in USA by air, when he dropped by parachute to organise the landing of R.34 at Mineola, 6 July 1919.

Fig. 50 Flight Lieutenant J E M Pritchard, RAF, the Officer in Charge of the flight trials.

Fig. 52 Flight Lieutenant Thomas and Air Commodore Maitland with Mrs Maxfield, wife of Commander Maxfield, USN, Captain-designate of ZR-2.

Fig. 53 Flt Lt Thomas, Sqn Ldr Hicks (an early airshipman) and Flt Lt Wann at a Howden sports meeting in which the US Naval Airship Detachment took part.

hardly doing justice to a subject 699 feet long and $85^1/_2$ feet in diameter.

Personnel were called to dinner at 7 o'clock in anticipation of calm air by 9pm, but at 7.15 their confidence was eroded by the appearance of the

> small, round, slightly bald and usually cheery Meteorological Officer [Mr. H. F. Jackson]. The observant noticed with alarm that he was in no way cheery. He looked at the fish as though he knew it were stale the while he lamented the lot of the meteorologist.

The reason was soon obvious, as the cooling air and unabated wind soon bore great billows of fog across the airfield, almost obscuring the beacon light on the top of the shed.

Even scientists can be superstitious, and Flight Lieutenant J. E. M. Pritchard, MA(Cantab), FRGS, OBE, AFC, closes his account thus:

> The worst had happened, the trial had to be postponed, R.38's persistent ill-luck has once again triumphed. The question - who is the Jona![sic]

Privately, and with justification, he may have had a shortlist of possible Jonahs - including some that were both high-ranking and non-flying.

XIII

Light as a Feather

At last, on 22 August, the frustrating wind relented and a relieved Met. Officer was able to predict a few comparatively settled days. The word went out by official and unofficial channels and the frantic preparations of the 18th were repeated. Rations for one day's flying were put on board and the chosen personnel packed their small-kit and handed in their valises and kitbags for transfer to Pulham by road. With the crew aboard at their landing stations to maintain trim, the gas and ballast were carefully adjusted to weigh off the ship to neutral buoyancy. The restraining trays of weights and fore and aft spring balances were cast off, and the 300 handlers took hold of the guys, strops and rails, and in strict silence marched the huge craft carefully along the centreline into the open. It was 6am.

It was a proud but sad moment for Air Commodore Edward Maitland, airship pioneer and the first holder of balloon, airship and aeroplane pilot licences. Born in 1880, he joined the Essex Regiment after graduating from Cambridge, and served in the South African War (1899-1902). Bored by peacetime soldiering, he developed an interest in ballooning, making a record journey, with two companions, from Crystal Palace to Russia in 1908 - a distance of 1,117 miles. An aeroplane which he built at his own expense was paid the compliment of being bought by the War Office, who also appointed him to command the Balloon School at Farnborough in 1909 and to the newly formed Air Battalion in 1910. On the formation of the Royal Flying Corps in 1913 he became Lieutenant Colonel Maitland, CO of No.1 Squadron (Airships). In 1914 (airships having been taken over by the Admiralty) he was gazetted to the Royal Naval Air Service as a Wing Commander in charge of kite (observation) balloons, in which post he carried out many experiments to improve safety - often at great personal risk. Particularly devoted to parachutes, he made many descents, including a 10,000 feet drop over London, earning the DSO for this work. Although he failed to convince the stubborn 'Boom' Trenchard to adopt them for aeroplanes, parachutes saved many valuable lives of balloon observers. Many thousands of aviators of a later generation owed their lives to his perseverance.

There was a rumour, reported in the American press, that ZR-2's kitten mascot 'Goldflake' had its personal parachute! This may not have been journalistic invention, as 'Brainy' Dobbs had used both his dog and a number of dead rabbits as research assistants in his parachute experiments.

Following a frustrating stint at an Admiralty desk, Maitland was appointed CO of the new airship station at Pulham for a year, until recalled to lead Britain's revived interest in rigid dirigibles. On the formation of the Royal Air Force on 1 April 1918 he became a Brigadier General and Supervisor of Airships. Never a man to stand on his dignity, he was happiest when he was directly involved in experiments and in flying his beloved airships. By frequent visits to airship works and stations, he was known and respected by everyone in the service. It surprised no one when he insisted on travelling as senior officer on R.34's very risky Atlantic crossing in 1919, although deferring to Major G. H. Scott as Captain.

Now, as Director of Airships, he was about to hand over the world's finest flying machine to the only country which could afford to operate it. With his dedication to lighter-than-air flight (perhaps obsessively) he must have felt that Britain was wantonly handing over a major national asset to a rival. The consolation was that the torch was being handed to believers in the cause. Walking with the Associated Press correspondent, he remarked proudly, 'Now she is as light as a feather'; and as the entire ship cleared the shed he added, 'She is beautiful'.

With the bow aligned to the light wind, the six motors were run up and the engine telegraphs were tested. With the handlers ready to compensate for changes in trim - and no doubt shy of the water ballast vents - Maitland climbed the short ladder to the control car, followed by Maxfield who had been saying goodbye to his wife and daughter.

After some last-minute changes, the complement of ZR-2 was now 27 Royal Air Force, 17 United States Navy, 3 National Physical Laboratory and 2 Royal Airship Works personnel.

At 7.10am the command 'Let go' and a unified push sent ZR-2 gently upwards. The engines were opened up, with a solitary US Navyman waving from the open cockpit at the extreme tail. Of those that watched the departure, one of the least happy was Lieutenant Commander R. E. Byrd. He had arrived from America on the *Olympic* on the previous Saturday and had planned to join the ship at

Howden. Missing his intended train on Monday, he had arrived at the airfield by taxi in time to watch in frustration (yet again) as Captain Wann rewarded the spectators and newsmen with two circuits, before setting off eastwards for a day of tests over the North Sea, during which they carried out the vital petrol consumption tests at various speeds up to 40 knots. Some limited turning trials were possible, but the NPL personnel were also involved in measuring relative airspeeds at different locations, such as aft of the engine radiators.

With a full day's work behind them, Captain Wann headed over the Norfolk coast towards Pulham, to be met by mist and low cloud fifteen miles from the base. From the dangerous height of 700 feet (just the length of the ship) it was impossible to see the ground, and so it was decided to wait off the coast until daybreak, using the time for further speed trials. For the tired crew it was a miserable night, as no sleeping bags had been issued and attempts to sleep were thwarted by attempts to restart a stubborn forward engine.

From 06.00 hours on Wednesday, 24 August, the fuel consumption tests were resumed and the last of the flight rations were eaten, somewhere in the vicinity of Howden. Someone on board dropped a stamped addressed letter, weighted by a bolt, at the village of South Cave; it was retrieved and posted. At noon ZR-2 reported her position as 28 miles off Felixstowe, and after a cautious probe towards Pulham she signalled at 13.15 that no landing would be attempted until the cloud height increased. The issue of 24 hour emergency rations at lunchtime was bad news for a tired crew which had already endured 30 hours of intermittent watchkeeping.

With the routine work completed, the time had come for the long-awaited and crucial full speed run. Above the clouds the weather was perfect, with a clear blue sky over dazzling white clouds below. It would first be necessary to find the speed and direction of the wind at operational height, in order to know their ground position after the trial. Descending cautiously to 1,000 feet over the sea they were able to find the Humber, which they followed to Howden, where Flight Lieutenant Little requested (by Aldis lamp) that a captive balloon should be flown to 3,000 feet, above cloud. By taking drift readings on this marker on three courses they could calculate the wind. He added that they would land at Howden rather than Pulham. At 16.30 a radio signal reported that the long-awaited full speed trials were in progress.

During all the speed and manoeuvring trials, Harry Bateman of the NPL had been stationed in the open rear cockpit, aft of the fins. Armed with two cameras, a notebook and a portable airspeed indicator, his task was to record the pressures shown on a series of water manometers (simple but accurate pressure gauges), which

Fig. 54 ZR-2 is coaxed from the Howden Twin Rigid Shed for its last flight on
23 August 1921

Fig. 55 The only known photograph of ZR-2 (note the American star) in flight over
Howden Airship Station.

Fig. 56 Parachutes of the 'Guardian Angel' type were available for all in R.38/ZR-2. This picture (actually in the keel of R.34) shows bunks, petrol tanks and an empty ballast bag. Two parachutes are stowed (foreground) beside the walkway. In an emergency a crewman would clip on and jump through the fabric envelope.

Fig. 58 Practice jumps were made from a captive balloon at Howden.

Fig. 57 Sgt Gary Gurowich models the parachute harness which he has made. He was fortunate not to be chosen for the final flight, as the crewmen who jumped fell into blazing petrol.

Fig. 59 United States Naval officers at Howden Airship Station. Commander Maxfield is third from the left.

Fig. 60 The RAF Trial Crew of R.38/ZR-2. A lucky few were omitted from the fatal flight to make way for the USN crewmen and the test observers.

were connected to tubes on the control surfaces. For the stressful full speed run the crew were ordered to their stations to report any damage as it occurred. Duffield of the NPL was in the keel forward of the control car, reading the airspeed on an accurate instrument forward of all obstructions. Pannell, with Pritchard assisting, was directing the sequence, and on Commander Campbell's suggestion he warned Bateman not to go to his station until the engine revs had stabilised and the ship was fully trimmed. A recent accident to the fins of R.36 had suggested that this was a danger zone in airships, and it was one of the main reasons for the NPL pressure tests.

At 1,800 revs on all engines the airspeed passed 52 knots (59.8 mph) and the nervous Bateman nipped aft to take 20 photographs of the manometer board. Returning forward to await the increase to 2,000 revs, he reported that many of the USN men had returned to the crew space between frames 7a and 7b - an unhealthy concentration of weight as well as a lack of vigilance. He heard Flight Lieutenant Little (the ship still being under RAF command) pass an order to resume landing stations, but he was not aware of it being implemented after he returned to his lonely outpost. Here he was joined by Corporal Walter Potter, RAF, who assisted him by making notes.

After fifteen minutes at 60 knots (69 mph), during which he detected nothing worse than the parting of two gas bag wires and two possible backfires, he started forward as the speed was reduced to about 45 - 50 knots. In the keel he met Maitland and Campbell, who were carrying out their own inspection. Campbell commented on the steadiness of the tail - always the most vulnerable member in an airship - but observed that the outer fabric forward of the fins would require taping to the bracing wires to stop it from flapping. Both men seemed relaxed and confident.

At 17.00 a signal was sent to the Air Ministry and to Pulham that ZR-2 would land at Howden about 19.30 and that the 200 soldiers sent from the Norwich garrison would not be required that night. In the relaxed atmosphere on board, a number of tired men had taken to their bunks or were chatting in the crew area.

At Howden, the intercepted messge was carried from the wireless cabin to Captain Kingston, acting C.O., by civilian worker William Joy.

A conference was in progress in the control car between Pritchard, Campbell, Maitland and Maxfield. The weather was favourable, there were some hours to daylight left, and there remained the question of ZR-2's ability to withstand rough weather. Would extreme control movements in the dense air of low altitude be equivalent to the rigours of an Atlantic storm? There was no positive answer, but the mere survival of such a test would be encouraging.

The pressure readings on the control surfaces would indicate the degree of stressing. They all knew the strictures imposed on a *height climber* flying at low altitude, just as the legendary Icarus had been warned not to take his wax-cemented wings too close to the sun. But would it be more prudent to risk damage in a controlled experiment near a convenient airship base than by chance over a hostile ocean?

For John Edward Maddock Pritchard, who had argued so strenuously against reckless shortcuts in the test programme, it was a personal as well as professional dilemma; he was committed to the Atlantic crossing and faced the danger either way. As the officer responsible for the trials he now went aft to brief the key observer, Harry Bateman, who had assumed with some relief that his work was done.

Flying over the sparsely populated Holderness Plain at about 54 knots (62 mph) and at altitudes between 1,500 and 2,500 feet, R.38/ZR-2 began a series of rudder movements of increasing magnitude.

The time was 17.27 hours.

If the ancient gods were watching, they may have called Icarus to the celestial window to watch the fun.

XIV

Icarus

Earlier in the long flight the rudder angle indicator in the control car had broken, so that Captain Wann could only assume that the rudders were responding to the amount of helm applied. In the rear cockpit the very busy Mr Bateman could estimate the degree of rudder displacement by observing marks on the control cables. The pressure readings on the manometers which he was photographing also gave an indication of the angles. His opinion supported Wann's later evidence that turns had been made first with 10° of rudder and later with 15° in each direction in turn. The elevators were being used only to maintain a mean altitude, but this still required considerable movement to counteract the hunting tendency.

Following the high speed test there was an air of confidence, even complacency, on board ZR-2. Those USN crewmen who were not detailed for specific duty had returned to the crew space or to the bunks distributed along the keel. They were happy that the gruelling flight would finish inside an hour and that the ship would then be theirs. The recently married men could look forward to seeing their wives again; and Chief Machinist's Mate R. M. Coons, who was about to follow their example, was showing them the engagement ring he had just bought. Bored with the conversation, Aviation Rigger Norman Otto Walker, a twenty year old Texan, made his way aft towards the tail cockpit, from which he enjoyed watching the scenery. He considered himself lucky to have been a last-minute replacement for Chief Machinist's Mate Sylvester Shields who had reported sick.

Leading Aircraftman Ernest Wynne Davies, RAF, was also looking for a vantage point, and he headed for the lower machine-gun pit which protruded as a shelf below the hull aft of Frame 10. Finding it occupied by Aircraftmen C. W. Penson and R. Withington, he looked over their shoulders for a few minutes and then turned to go forward again.

At 17.34, in the wireless cabin abaft the control car, Flying Officer Victor H. Wicks acknowledged a routine contact signal from Howden.

* * *

By now the cloud was broken in places and ZR-2 was approaching Hull from the North East, perhaps in farewell to a city that had given the airshipmen hospitality and friendship. By coincidence or design they passed close to the village of Sutton, where some of the American officers had been entertained by Mr and Mrs Edwin Robson of Sutton House a few days before. Having just married a daughter to an Army officer, and as four daughters remained, it would be natural to have eligible young officers on the visiting list, apart from the traditional courtesies of Yorkshire hospitality. In war-shattered Britain, eligible young men were very scarce.

Shortly after ZR-2 had passed, a small boy fielded a letter attached to a streamer and delivered it to a house at nearby Haworth. It was from Flight Lieutenant Godfrey Thomas (holder of the DFC for sinking a U-boat) to his fiancée.

On a course of approximately 239° magnetic ZR-2 emerged from cloud, heading over Alexandra Dock. The helm movements which now followed did not appreciably alter the course, as the reversals cancelled each other before the ship had time to turn. The intention was simply to simulate the stresses expected from rough weather.

To the thousands of people going home from work, taking the sun on the waterfront, or brought outdoors by the rumble of the six Sunbeam Cossack engines, she was a fine sight, graceful and silver in the sunlight. To young Charles Ayre, who had just left his father's motorboat *Kitty* grounded at the pier, she was:

> . . . a truly magnificent sight . . . like some giant silver
> monster. The control cabin, glistening in the sun,
> reminded me of the ends of the electric trams which
> were much in evidence at that time.

A number of citizens enjoying the evening sun on the promenade deck over Victoria Pier had the best view as the huge vessel moved from left to right to pass a few hundred yards in front of them. At about 2,500 feet altitude the details were clear and some observers could see men in the control car. Thousands of workers on their way home, many on bicycles in this flat city, paused to watch as the impressive craft appeared momentarily between buildings.

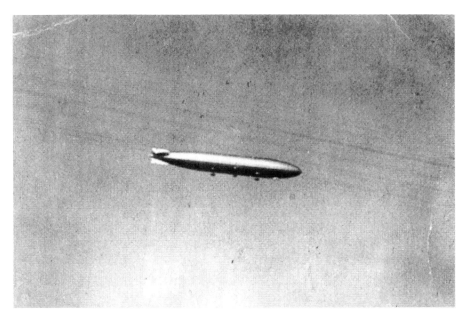

Fig. 61 The last known photograph of R.38/ZR-2. The donor, who found it in a drawer, was unaware of the airship's identity, but was sure it was taken over Hull.

Fig. 62 This photograph was taken by an unknown aerial cameraman from the approximate point at which R.38/ZR-2 broke up. Victoria Pier with its promenade deck, towards which the stricken airship veered, is visible behind the ferryboat.
(Photo: Hull Central Library)

Fig. 63 The Promenade Deck on Victoria Pier, crowded at time of accident.
(Photo: Hull Central Library)

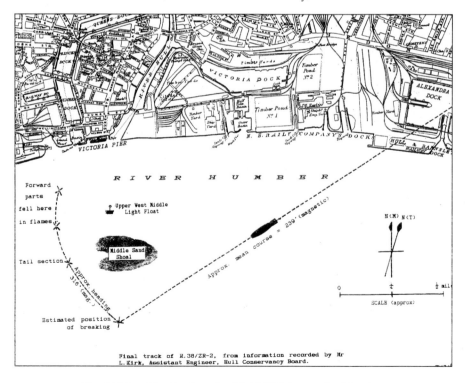

Fig. 64 Map. The final track of R.38/ZR-2 over the Humber.

Others rushed out of houses and shops or went to upper windows for a better view. Among them were off-duty members of the Howden Detachment, enjoying a final day out in Hull.

We cannot know if the decision to order the final 15° rudder movements was prompted by the sight of clear water and a safe testing area ahead; or whether it was an Icarus-like abandonment of caution, born of the success of the speed trial, with perhaps a desire to show Hull some real flying.

The time was 17.37 on 24 August 1921.

* * *

The watchers formed varying impressions of what happened next, but all remember sudden changes in direction and attitude of the ship. All agree that a crease appeared diagonally across the hull towards the after end. To ten-year-old Norman Forester it looked like water running down the side. Another thought it was like a 'frown on a man's forehead'. Chief Machinist's Mate Charles W. Cass, USN, on leave in Hull before joining the ship at Pulham, had the unscientific but graphic impression of 'a great wrinkle, like a twisted and rolled newspaper in her outer cover, midship.' Most of the waterfront observers remember a cloud of vapour which to F. W. Daddy at Beeton Street on Holderness Road seemed to turn the ship from silver to dark grey. This was almost certainly water ballast being discharged and vapourising in the turbulence around the hull. It could also have been petrol from ruptured tanks as the crease now widened and the airship 'cracking open like an egg' disgorged objects and men. The nose dropped sharply, then parted and fell.

Ex-RAF Major A. C. Hartley was driving his Overland car quickly towards Paragon Station to catch the 5.40pm Hornsea train, but slowed down at Monument Bridge to peer under the hood with professional interest at the state-of-the-art flying machine. Passing Anne Street, still in a hurry, he saw crowds rush to the corner and look upwards, so he stopped, reversed and got out of the car to see the two sections drifting apart with a parachute in the air between them.

At the other end of the long street which ran from the riverside to Hull Royal Infirmary (then in Prospect Street), the eight and nine year old Howard and Ivy Grainger had charge of their baby brother Douglas while their mother went to buy bread. They heard and then saw the airship - 'a beautiful sight' - as it appeared over the rooftops. They saw the hull buckle, the ends dropping, and fire and explosion erupting as the parts separated. Heedless of possible danger or the certain 'rollicking' which would ensue on their return, they set off at best speed down Prospect Street with baby Douglas bouncing before them in his pushchair.

The suddenness of the breakup confused onlookers. To some, the ends of the hull folded downwards before parting. Others thought they rose, but it is most likely in view of the violent rudder movements and the memories of survivors that it *writhed* as girders and wires progressively parted, taking various attitudes and headings in quick succession. Only one witness - J. W. Innes in Scale Lane - records the hush as 'engines suddenly stopped . . . not slightest doubt about this as change to silence from roar of engines most noticeable.'

The front portion had caught fire either just before parting or immediately afterwards - the witnesses disagree - but the ignition was followed by a colossal explosion as the hydrogen from ruptured gas cells was rapidly stirred into the turbulent air around the heaving wreck.

Further objects dropped, including petrol tanks which spread burning fuel over the water, into which crew and wreckage descended. Police Constable Skinner, picking himself up after the first explosion, had the impression of *three* men hanging from one parachute. Henry Branton on nearby Riverside Quay, also prostrated by the blast, thought there were only two men. If more crewmen jumped, as some witnesses reported, they were soon engulfed in the smoke and flame and quickly overtaken by the falling forward section, still over five hundred feet long. The second massive blast which now followed within seconds spewed further fuel and oil over the surface to encircle the wreckage.

In the city, windows shattered over a wide area and many people were cut by flying glass or knocked off their feet by the blasts. Mariana Brown died of shock, the only non-flying fatality. A pram with a sleeping baby was flung to one end of a garden. In Porter Street a barber closed shop, too shaken to continue shaving. A general stampede towards the river blocked the approach roads.

Those on Victoria Pier and its environs experienced the double shocks of the explosion as well as the visual horror, made worse by the stricken ship veering sharply in their direction before hitting the water in two pieces. Charles Ayre, with clear recall many years later, takes up the story:

> Two terrific explosions rent the air, the impact of which seemed to tear my head from my shoulders at this time and I thought it prudent to move as the whole horrible inferno was coming to where I was standing.

Many others were of the same opinion and in the frantic exodus from Victoria Pier people were knocked down by the second

Fig. 65 While petrol still burns on the water, rescuers head for the wreckage. On the left is the *Queen* (buoy yacht) with the tug *Spurn* and steam survey launch *W.S. Wright*. Some smaller craft reached the survivors in the stranded tail section.

Fig. 66 No photographs exist of the actual crash, but a postcard publisher commissioned Ern Shaw, a cartoonist, to superimpose drawings of the sequence on views of Hull, based on eyewitness accounts.

Fig. 67 Mr Harry Bateman of the National Physical Laboratory (seen here in Royal Naval uniform) was stationed in the tail cockpit during the manoeuvring trials.

Fig. 68 This tail turret on R.33 (later removed) was only slightly more exposed than Harry Bateman's station on R.38/ZR-2.

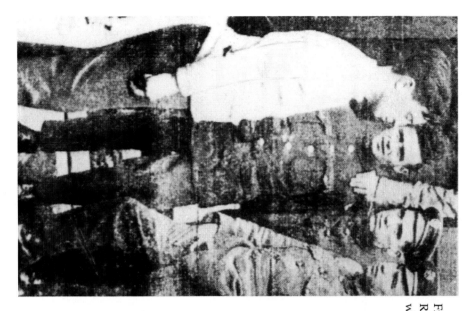

Fig. 69 Corporal Walter Potter, RAF, who did not even get wet.

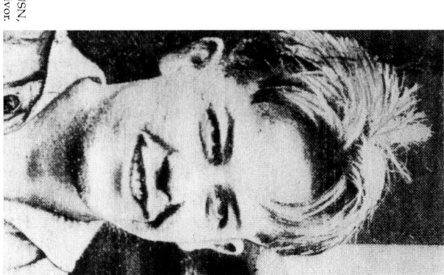

Fig. 70 Norman O. Walker, USN, the sole American survivor.

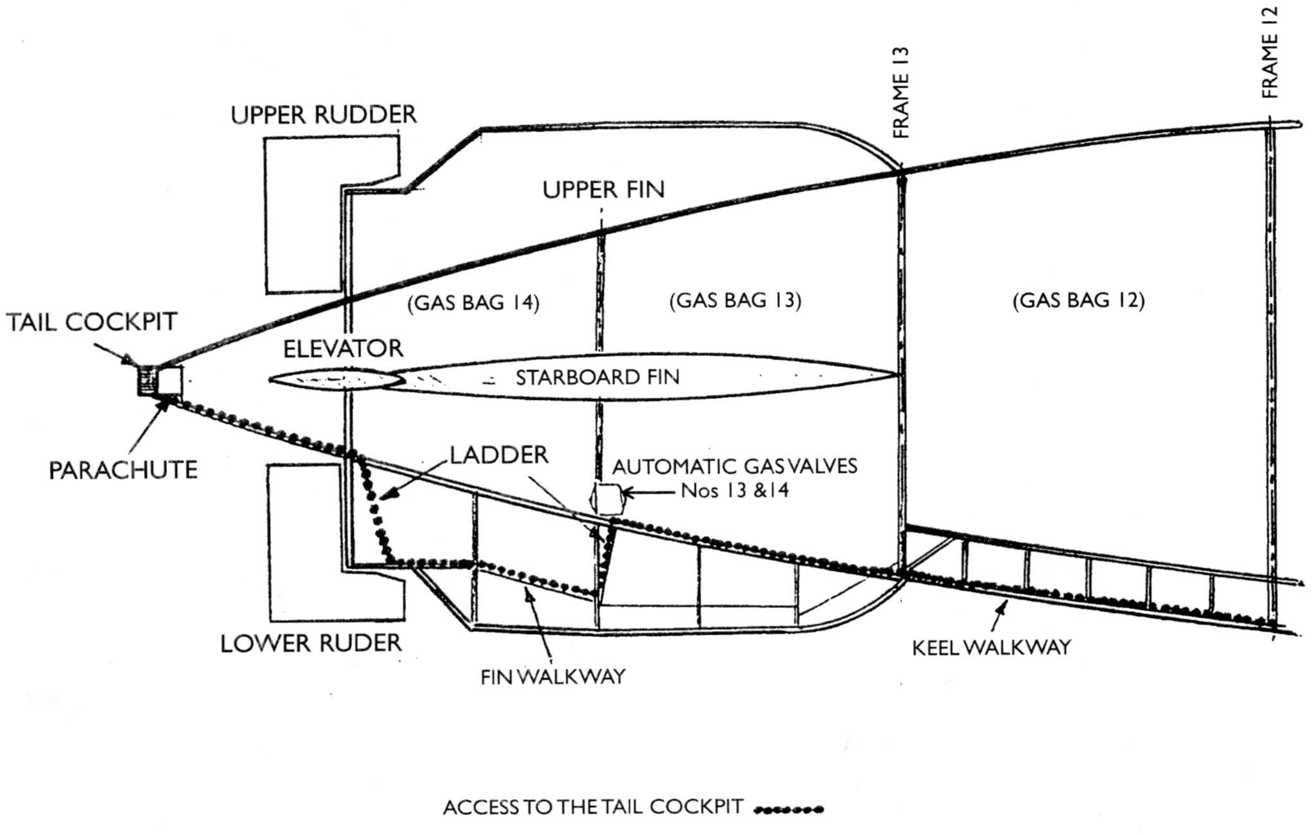

ACCESS TO THE TAIL COCKPIT •••••••

Fig. 71 Diagram

Fig. 72 Rescuers vainly search the stranded tail for more survivors. Harry Bateman's tangled parachute remains trapped in the bracing wires of the fin on the right.

Fig. 73 Next morning, the search for bodies.

detonation or by the rush. Among them were the Wooddisse children who had been horrified by the fall of a parachutist into the flames and were heading for a tram to take them home. Charles Ayre

> . . . ran faster than I have ever done since, until I was able to timidly look over my shoulder. . . .Flames and smoke stretched far out along the bank for hundreds of yards. I noticed several airmen in parachutes descend directly into this fire.

The screams which had accompanied the disaster - both from the crowd and from the stricken airship - now gave way to complete silence as the last few minutes of the tragedy were played out. With the shattered forward section already in the water and surrounded by flames and smoke, the stunned crowd watched the comparatively gentle descent of the rear section as it turned towards the city and came to rest on a sandbank. The Woodisse children, now waiting at a tram stop, had an impression of 'one man on the tailplane and one in a parachute.'

* * *

On board the after section of the broken dirigible four men were still alive.

Harry Bateman, absorbed in his work, was not immediately disturbed by a series of lateral shocks followed by longitudinal jerks, which he put down to an engine clutch slipping badly. The thrust wires from the rear engines were attached at Frame 11, from which the longitudinals ran straight back to the tail, virtually telegraphing engine behaviour to the trained ear of a man who had lectured on engines during his wartime RNAS service. A few seconds later:

> Then loud cracks which could only be the breaking of girders were heard in rapid succession. I jumped to my feet but overbalanced due to the large pitch of the tail portion (tail down). My notebook and watch and other instruments were scattered in all directions. Then I realised I must get out of the ship with all possible speed. Potter rushed forward to his parachute position but mine was in the cockpit. My parachute was attached to a spare harness but I was already equipped with harness and in my haste, I attached myself with one of my loops without removing the other harness.

There was still some cloud below, and he had been too intent on his work to notice whether they were over water. He looked for his kapok waistcoat but could not see it. The movement was now violent and there were more cracks. It was decision time.

> I jumped, but the spare harness became entangled with the bracing wires in the cockpit. I managed to struggle back to the cockpit and threw the harness and parachute case overboard with my right hand while hanging on with my left hand. I must have left the parachute rope [the rope between the harness and the canopy] resting on a small aluminium hook . . . for, on letting myself fall, the rope jammed into the hook and I was hanging about a yard below the cockpit. Although I struggled to climb up again I could not free myself.

Although Bateman could see dark grey smoke about the hull forward of the fins, he was still not aware of what had happened to the ship. He had not even heard any explosions. Three other men were only too aware, especially Ernest Davies. He was approaching Frame 10 when the walkway buckled under his feet and then parted. He glimpsed Lieutenant Commander Coil stagger in the next bay as the forward part separated and rapidly drifted away. The explosion which followed in a few seconds shook and stunned him, and he was conscious of being drenched in petrol. Surrounded by broken girders and tangled wires, he was next aware of trying to keep his head above water and to fight his way to the top of the envelope.

Walter Potter was in the cockpit when the break occurred. He immediately climbed down the ladder in the lower fin to reach the walkway and to head for his parachute station. Here he was met by a dazed Norman Walker who had been knocked down by the sudden pitching and had narrowly missed decapitation by snapping cables. It was soon obvious to them that there was no salvation forward: the walkway was blocked by broken girders and beyond that there was daylight. For want of a better option they climbed into the cockpit, from which they looked down at the hapless Harry Bateman dangling a few feet below. Potter may have had mixed feelings about Bateman's suggestion that they should jump together on one parachute, but it was an academic proposal as the tangled gear could not be freed. Instead, they hauled him back to the edge of the cockpit, where he hung on as the rear section glided quite gently at an angle of about 20° tail down, before levelling out as if under control for touchdown.

During the descent they could not see much of the forward portion, which had already reached the water with a second massive detonation. Its position, about 100 yards to landward, was surrounded by burning oil and petrol and several floating tanks. Pieces of fabric were still falling and a parachute with another unopened one entangled with it made a slow descent, landing its two passengers gently among the flames.

The reluctant riders on the tail made a soft landing as the lower fin ploughed into a sandbank. Norman Walker, who had jumped just before the impact, was surprised to find himself submerged only to the waist. They had been remarkably lucky. Their section of the airship had landed on the Middle Sand - a shoal just off Victoria Pier - and as the tide was almost at full ebb there was little depth and no appreciable current to sweep them away. However, the shallowness prevented the larger and faster vessels from reaching the trio, and they had to wait until a small boat was launched: 'an agonising wait of ten minutes, wondering whether the blazing petrol would reach the ship first.'

At the pier many potential rescuers were also wondering about the petrol, until a shout of 'Aren't you putting off to them then?' from someone in the otherwise silent crowd started a concerted move towards the wreckage by all available craft - mainly tugs - which were sufficiently steamed up and manned. There was understandable hesitation about approaching the flame-encircled bow wreckage, but among the first to reach the stranded stern was the Humber Conservancy Board's steam launch *Pilot* with John William Osborne in charge. He immediately deployed the crew to hack open the fabric with knives. In this way they found and extricated the ensnared Ernest Davies just before the wreck shifted and rolled in the slight current. They could not reach the entangled American crewman who appeared, mercifully, to be either unconscious or dead. Two bodies in American uniform floated in the water, out of reach.

Arthur Hewitt, then an 18 year old crewman of the paddle tug *Stephen Gray*, was alone on board when the first explosion brought him up on to the quay.

> I saw the airship split in two and then there was another explosion and the parts fell in the Humber near the sandbanks off the Corporation Pier. We were detailed to proceed to the wreckage as soon as our crew were on board, to try to pick up any survivors; however, we were preceded by other small craft, one being a tug named the *Tyne* which had picked up some bodies and was taking them to the Pier.

He also saw the tug *Marksman* and the *Pilot* launch, and the Humber Conservancy buoy vessel *Queen*. Photographs taken during the rescue attempts show a number of craft including the steam survey launches *W. S. Wright* and *Spurn* together with several rowing boats.

One of the craft warily circling the flames at last found an opening and was in time to pull two men from the vicinity of the control car before it turned over and sank. One of them, USN Lieutenant Charles Little, who had so recently married at Brough, died before reaching the pier. The other was the Captain, flight Lieutenant Wann, stunned, injured and burned but miraculously alive. He was assisted ashore, examined and dispatched to hospital by Lieutenant William Taylor of USN Medical Corps, just arrived by taxi from his house in Beverley Road. The excited and breathless Grainger children were in time to see the survivors and the first bodies being landed, to be consigned to the ultimate care of their father Harry, who as Head Porter of the Infirmary was also keeper of the hospital mortuary. It was many years before young Howard was able to correct his childhood impression that he had witnessed the landing of 'Captain One' - presumably an esoteric airship rank!

As each of the five survivors were landed - Aircraftman Ernest Davies insisting on walking off the tug *Norman* - there were cheers. Dr G. W. Lilley, who had rushed from his home in Williamson Street, spoke to Davies who was - 'smoking a cigarette and said he was all right; but he had been in the water and appeared as if he wanted to walk away.' To a reporter Davies said, 'I'm too ill to talk, but I will say we've had a terrible time.' Dr Lilley called Police Constable Skinner, and the confused airman was taken to the Infirmary.

Norman Otto Walker, completely unhurt but soaked - and the sole American survivor - was taken to a police cell to dry out; and here he was found by a relieved CMM Sylvester Shields, whom he had replaced in the crew. Among numerous small errors in the hastily written press reports he was named *N.O'Walker*, which may account for the report of his death which reached the American newspapers.

The probing of the wreckage continued as long as the now flooding tide would permit, but there were to be no more cheers.

* * *

Two would-be rescuers had intimate knowledge of the layout of ZR-2 as they were designated crew members. Chief Machinist's Mates Charles Broome and Charles Cass were on the Atlantic crew list, but not being required for the trial flight they were in Hull, the former with his English wife and new baby. Broome watched the dirigible as she approached from the northeast, thinking that the sudden rudder movements were peculiar. As the ship disintegrated he ran to the pier in time to join one of the tugs which had sufficient crew and was in steam. When it grounded at the edge of the shoal he jumped into one of the rowing boats heading for the unburned tail section. While others hacked at the fabric he swam to the cockpit - recently vacated by the three survivors - and entered the hull through the tailfin. Working his way between the outer cover and the three remaining gasbags, he swam about in the gloom until he found a body which he pulled out to the rescuers. It was Flight Lieutenant Montagu. CMM Cass had also joined a tug which nosed up to the tail section as the tide rose, but the increasing current of the flooding tide, rolling and shifting the wreck, prevented a further search.

* * *

One man who had a unique view of the entire sequence was Mr L. Kirk, Assistant Engineer of the Hull Conservancy Board, on the buoy yacht *Queen* lying close to the eastern corner of the Hull and Barnsley Railway's Riverside Quay. With responsibility for mooring the buoys and light vessels in the capricious channels of the Humber estuary, he had a professional eye for marks and bearings and clearly registered the movements of the approaching airship.

> I first sighted the airship above the East Coal Transporter on the Hull and Barnsley Quay, travelling approximately in a S 59°W direction. After she had travelled about 7,000 feet she was observed to be turning acutely and at the same time breaking.

As a keen photographer, and ex-president of Hull Photographic Society, he had a camera on board and was able to take three photographs immediately after the two portions of wreckage hit the water. With professional detachment he memorised the position of the breakup and resting places of the wreckage. These he confirmed by taking bearings on the Clock Tower, Riverside Quay, Trinity Church and Earles' (shipyard) Crane.

Not only was Kirk able to produce a map of the event for the subsequent inquiry and the marking of the wreckage for navigation and salvage, but his factual and detailed account (preserved in the Hull Conservancy Board's archives) remains the best guide to the true sequence of the accident. It has been invaluable in giving a framework to the conflicting - and understandably emotional - reports of observers given to the Press immediately after the disaster.

XV

Sympathy, Sensation and Salvage

With the tide flooding strongly and soon to cover the twisted remains entirely, the immediate tasks were to mark the wreck as a hazard to shipping and to commence the search for the dead - and for clues to the cause of the accident. These necessities were set in motion within the hour.

At about 7pm the Secretary of the Humber Conservancy Board, Alfred W. Franklin, was asked by his namesake Commander Franklin, the Naval District Intelligence Officer, to make all arrangements for the marking and lighting of the wreckage as he 'was not able to do so himself'. The Secretary hastened to comply, engaging the Humber sloop *Nellie and May* by verbal agreement with Mr W. H. Barraclough, the owner. Shortly after midnight the substantial improvised light vessel was moored to the northwest of the wreckage. A *Warning to Mariners* notice was rushed to the printers.

The news hit Howden quickly and hard. At the Airship Station the Acting C.O. (Captain Kingston) was informed by telephone and the news quickly spread through the waiting landing party. The newspaper report of a last frantic wireless message 'Ship broken falling' is not recorded in the Howden radio operator's log and is probably a journalistic invention; but it made a hero of Flying Officer Victor Wicks for reputedly sticking to his post to send it. In Howden town, which had hosted airshipmen and women for four years and in which many married servicemen and civilian workers lived, there was profound shock, as they had last seen 'their' airship during its brief appearance about 4pm that day. They received the news verbally, as personnel from the camp spread the word - with the usual inaccuracies and hearsay which attend a calamity and which inevitably colour the press accounts. In those days the Hull and Barnsley Railway still passed through Howden town, while the rival

North Eastern Railway station was closer to the airfield. People gathered at the Wellington Hotel, a favoured rendezvous of the airmen. Mr Hewson, the landlord, did his best to relay such items as filtered through or could be obtained by frequent calls to the Hull newspaper offices. The next train from Howden to Hull carried a number of passengers amongst whom were friends and relations of crew members. They included the wife of an American 'officer', as the *Eastern Morning News* of the following morning reported, with genteel emotion:

> This lady was only confined three weeks ago and despite her delicate state of health she took the next train to Hull. Her anxiety was frantic and it is feared it would not be alleviated upon her arrival at Hull, for she would only learn that her husband was one of the victims. Her friends at Howden became considerably alarmed when she had not returned home at a late hour last night.

She was in fact the American wife of CMM W. A. Julius, carrying the infant Dorothea Leontine Louise in her arms. In Hull she pleaded in vain to be allowed on board one of the boats still probing the wreckage. Also at the pier was the Yorkshire wife of CMM W. J. Steele (née Joyce Elizabeth Hannam) who had married in Leeds on 4 July, too recently to be sent to America with the other brides. Soon discovered by the newsmen, she contributed a suitably pathetic and newsworthy quote by repeatedly crying 'Where's my Billy?'.

The same paper also recorded that:

> News of the disaster cast a gloom over Brough, where several of the officers had resided during their training at Howden.

In neighbouring Goole, likewise a temporary host town to airshipmen and the permanent home of civilian workers, the *Goole Times* had received the news within twenty minutes of the crash. As they were not due to publish until Friday, they posted a bulletin in their window. It was soon surrounded by a deeply shocked crowd.

* * *

As soon as *Kitty* could be refloated on the rising tide, Charles Ayre and his father put off to view the wreckage. Their shallow draft enabled them to move among the tangled mass on the sandbank.

> As we were manoeuvring into a narrow fairway, we
> were hailed by a tall, impressive-looking officer in
> USA uniform and he asked if we would care to help
> get the bodies of airmen out of the debris. Of course
> we agreed to help.

The officer was Commander Richard E. Byrd, USN, who had so
narrowly missed ZR-2's departure from Howden, and by this chance
survived to achieve fame for his pioneer Polar aeroplane flights.
Now, as the senior US Naval representative at the scene, he
contracted *Kitty* for a fee of £5 a day for the duration of the search.

There was to be one sad posthumous message from the ship that
day. On Anlaby Road, downwind of ZR-2's final track, an elderly
gentleman was cycling home when the crash occurred. As he looked
in the direction of the smoke a large piece of silk with a letter
attached landed at his feet. It was addressed to the parents of a crew
member and must have been written earlier with the possibility of
death in mind - a not uncommon practice among servicemen. The
letter was forwarded and acknowledged with gratitude.

* * *

Thursday morning brought a huge crowd to the waterfront to
gaze at the visible remains of the after section, now stripped naked
by the flood and ebb of the fierce Humber tide. Small craft circled
the wreck sites and searched for souvenirs until warned off for their
own safety. A contingent of reporters, press photographers and
cinema newsreel cameramen were more persistent, until their
shallow-draught launch was requisitioned by service officers and
salvors who were debating the best method of recovery. The
pressmen turned their attention to the crowd, finding many accounts
and opinions to enliven the somewhat staid and conventional pages
of the *Hull Daily Mail* and the *Eastern Morning News* for several days.
The former was at pains to point out that it had included a paragraph
on the disaster in the previous evening's special edition - rather at
variance with the glowing account of the flight which had appeared
in the earlier editions. In London and other world capitals the news
hit the front pages, and opinions were sought from prominent
personages about the cause of the disaster. Salvage suggestions were
also freely available, including the unlikely idea of attaching the
wreck to the Humber sloop *Doris* and lifting it on the rising tide for a
tow to the Old Harbour.

At Hull Royal Infirmary Dr Levine stated that the injured
survivors were 'as well as could be expected.' In view of the nature
of the disaster they were probably a lot better than anyone could

have expected, but he was later pressed for a more detailed appraisal, revealing that Flight-Captain (sic) Wann had abrasions and a cut head and was 'very poorly'. Ernest Davies, who had tried to walk away after rescue, had been treated for a cut forehead and wrist. Lieutenant Little, USN, had been 'dead on arrival'.

* * *

Early on Friday morning the tug *Stephen Gray* was dispatched with a consort to King George Dock where they took in tow the 80 ton floating crane, known locally as *The Bull*, and positioned it at the wreck site to grapple for the pieces, with *Kitty* in attendance on her gruesome commission. The salvage sloop *Doris* was moved upstream and dropped down on the tide as close to the wreckage as possible. When sufficient material had been collected on the float or *Doris* or the quarter decks of the tugs, they edged their way to Riverside Quay, where the tangled mass of ribs, wires, fabric, tanks, engines and instruments was heaped up for investigation. Then with *Kitty* assisting by laying out the grapnel, they resumed their grim fishing.

While the practicalities were being dealt with, as was to be expected in a functioning and busy port, confusion multiplied in Service circles. With the cream of two airship services in the Royal Infirmary or City mortuaries or somewhere in the river, and with the international aspects of the incident already looming, someone with prestige had to be seen to be in charge. Accordingly, Air Vice Marshall Vyell Vyvyan, DSO, Air Officer Commanding Coastal Area, was installed in an office in the Vittoria Hotel overlooking the wreck site. One might have to search hard for any previous airship connection, but rank and office determine many things. It is of passing interest that he had entered the Royal Air Force by way of the Royal Navy, having seen service on the Naval expedition against the King of Benin in 1897 and also at the Dardanelles in 1915, as well as holding a number of Staff appointments. He had been one of the regular officers appointed to inject naval standards into the infant RNAS, and as a figurehead he was suitably decorated, with the Legion of Honour and the Orders of St. Anne, Rising Sun, American DSO, and Grand Cordon of the Redeemer. He does appear to have had diving experience, on the strength of which he vetoed the offer by the Hull and Barnsley Railway's diver to assist in the salvage because of the hazards of tide and tangled wreckage. For technical backup his Staff Officer was Wing Commander Cave-Brown-Cave who was a practical engineer with long experience of airships and who had been one of the designers of the *Submarine Scout* blimps. Major G. H. Scott, OBE, commander of R.34 on its double Atlantic crossing and one of the few rigid airship pilots remaining, was also dispatched to Hull to look for clues among the salvaged remains. The Royal Air Force officers did not 'live over the shop', preferring the more luxurious Royal Station Hotel to the ageing Vittoria.

Also on the scene but keeping a low profile were Messrs Randle and Gerrish, representing the builders and to assist with identification of the salvaged parts of the airship.

Reading through the files of the Humber Conservancy Board (which is now absorbed by Associated British Ports) one senses the frustration which Mr Franklin, Conservancy Secretary, must have endured. He expeditiously dealt with the immediate navigation requirements, including the publication of *Notice to Mariners (No.65)* of the 25th August, 1921 - headed *Airship ZR-2* - giving the location of the wreck, the position of the Marking Vessel and warning of drifting wreckage. He had approved the suggestion from Mr Mumby and Mr Holland at the Pilot Office that their flag should be flown at half mast as a mark of respect. He now had to attend to the legal and financial aspects. The matter of salvage will illustrate the difficulties.

Early on the Thursday morning he received a telegram from W. M. Loveridge of West Hartlepool; 'Have dispersers available for R.38 if required.' He telephoned the offer to Commander Franklin, Naval District Intelligence Officer, who passed it on to the Air Ministry presumably through Air Vice Marshall Vyvyan. At 4.05 pm the NDIO replied that the local representatives of the Air Ministry had made local arrangements for salvage. Franklin (of Hull Conservancy) now had to write to Loveridge to decline his offer, incidentally admitting that he *did not know* what the alternative arrangements were. One would have expected him to have been told, as a matter of courtesy if not necessity.

It transpired that Air Vice Marshall Vyvyan had contracted directly with the firm of R. and A. Leggot who were at work salving a vessel at the mouth of Old Harbour, and also with the North Eastern Railway's Dredging Department. By some arrangement *The Bull* and its attendant tugs were included. The following Sunday (28 August) Commodore Sir F. W. Young, KBE, RNR, arrived in Hull to assume control of the operations, followed by his salvage vessel *Reindeer* the next day. The *Hull Daily Mail* also noted the presence on the *Doris* of 'Air Commander Brooke Poppam (sic), Commander Byrd, Commander Newton White (representing Rear Admiral C. Neblick, U.S.A.), Commanders Regan and De Levene.'

If Mr Secretary Franklin had now a mind to wash his hands of the matter, it was not to be. With overall legal responsibility for navigation in the Humber (by the Humber Conservancy Act of 1898) and as the recognised local authority, he was obliged to process a multitude of incidents. This he did with meticulous care, even noting and filing the gist of all relevant telephone calls and verbal exchanges in handwritten memos. But verbal agreements, even between gentlemen, do not necessarily pay bills, so on the 27th Mr Barraclough was given a contract of hire for the *Nellie and May* at £3 per day of 24 hours, backdated to 8 pm on 24 August.

Then commenced a classic example of passing the buck - or more exactly the pound sterling - as the United States had not officially accepted the airship at the time of the accident. Softened by expressions of regret and sympathy (at least initially), requests for financial responsibility were bandied between Humber Conservancy, the Royal Navy, the Air Ministry and the many claimants for damages. In a way, it reflected the confusion about the entire R.38 episode - an airship designed by the Admiralty for the Royal Navy, adopted by the Royal Air Force, sold to the United States Navy, flown and crashed by a mixed crew of the RAF, USN and civilians.

* * *

The flooding tide had quickly dislodged loose and buoyant equipment from the wreckage, and together with items and bodies which had fallen during the breakup, swept them at speed towards Goole. Along the way, some came ashore or rested in eddies or in the mud. Twice a day the sad flotsam changed direction until picked up by ships, police, or souvenir hunters. With only three bodies so far in the City Mortuary in Castle Street and in the Royal Infirmary there was obviously much unpleasantness still to come, but seafaring people have a respect for the dead and it was hoped that all the victims would be recovered from the river. Meanwhile one reporter had sufficient material to compensate for grey years of ambulance chasing.

PATHETIC SCENES AT THE MORTUARY

VICTIMS TERRIBLE INJURIES

(The first line was lost due to a compositor's error, but it continues ..)

. . . witnessed by the crowds at the Pier and by a large gathering at the gates of the mortuary. Two bodies arrived there about seven o'clock, and the nature of the injuries suggested a terrible fate.

The faces were badly burned, but in the dead men's pockets waterproof wallets were found establishing their identity.

The first three recovered were identified as Captain (sic) Montagu, the RAF navigator, and Lieutenants Esterley and C. G. Little, USN. Their injuries and wallet contents were reported in considerable detail, suggesting that Mr Ernest Dougherty, Mortuary Caretaker (or possibly a police officer) was on good terms with the press. Lieutenant Esterley's arms were burned and his clothing saturated with petrol and water. His skull was broken.

> A parachute strap was fastened tightly round his body and it can be surmised that disaster overtook him before he could leave the ship. . . . A remarkable thing was that Mr Esterley's wrist watch was still going. A photograph of two bonny young children was found in the dead man's wallet. . . .
> . . . in (his) pocket was found a curious talisman - one popular among American airmen - the bone from a graveyard rabbit, worn for good luck or bad luck (sic).

A less sentimental task was the recovery of items which might throw some light on the cause of the crash. The Humber Conservancy notice had warned of floating wreckage, and this was supplemented by requests to report anything found which might have originated in the airship.

First to respond was the sailing sloop *Sylvia* (Mr Richardson, Master) docking at Goole on the morning after the accident. She had recovered some articles in the vicinity of the crash, but being on the flood tide, with a following wind, she had continued her journey until able to report to Mr Colquhoun, at the Humber Conservancy Board's Goole office. He wrote immediately to his Hull headquarters.

> . . . Mr Richardson . . . picked up the following articles:-
> Lifebuoy; Officer's cap; petrol tank clock gauge; complete shaving and toilet outfit in strong leather case; leather bound book fastened with steel clasps; Official book of instructions issued by American Air Ministry.
> Mr Richardson, who I understand hopes to berth his vessel at Messrs Williamson's Wharf, Old Harbour, Hull, about 4pm on Saturday 27th, further informs he is desirous of handing over the aforementioned articles to the proper authority.
> The sloop 'Sylvia' is owned by Mr Hodgson, Accountant, Trinity House Lane, Hull.

The methodical Secretary Franklin annotated the letter with the action to be taken, namely: 'Write Comm. Franklin (NDIO), Acknowledge, Write A.M.' but spoke personally to his namesake for speed, as other articles had been found by *Queen, W. S. Wright* and *Spurn*, including a large case of 60 maps, sodden but legible, and now spread out to dry over the Board Room furniture.

During the next few days conflicting instructions were given for recovery of evidence. On Friday, the NDIO advised that notifications of finds were to be addressed to the Royal Air Force Staff Officer in the Vittoria Hotel, 'who will arrange for collection of the articles'. On Saturday the District Intelligence Officer at Howden (RN or RAF not specified) instructed that material should be deposited at Naval H.Q. 4, West Parade, Hull. As this was a rented office it seems to have been an impractical suggestion, and by Sunday Air Vice Marshal Vyvyan had conceded (rather clumsily),

> Any bulky articles like the petrol tank, I should be obliged if you could send to the N.E.Rly Shed, where the remains of the Zeppelin (sic) wreckage is being dumped by the Floating Crane.

Meanwhile *The Bull* had continued its grim angling, aided by the Ayres, father and son, in *Kitty*.

> Our job was to take the grapnel iron which was a series of steel hooks fastened together in a cluster and tow it along the bed of the river until it caught up with the wreckage. We would then pass the line over to a large floating crane which in turn would heave the tangled mass onto the deck of the crane. In this manner we were able to retrieve the unfortunate victims who were entangled in the wreckage.

Charles Ayre was impressed by the dedication of the Americans who

> . . . would not let up for one instant. They brought out the searchlights and shone them on the water all through the nights and indeed they were long nights. I remember one day when the recovery of the dead was proving difficult Commander Byrd said 'The eyes of the whole world are upon this project and we must have all our dead'.

Commander Byrd was in constant attendance during the salvage operations together with other USN officers.

There was a moving incident when he stood in the cockpit of our launch as the crane slowly heaved a bunch of wreckage out of the water and entangled in the debris was the body of his friend, and as the crane continued to heave the poor victim's sodden clothes began to tear away, revealing his lower limbs. Commander Byrd quickly peeled off his uniform jacket and wrapped it around the body of his dead comrade until they were able to lay him gently down on the cockpit locker. He stood there with his hands upon the body with tears in his eyes until we got back to the pier.

The work became increasingly unpleasant as time passed and the summer temperature added to the horrors of mutilation. One foggy morning a passing boat told them that they suspected a floating body upstream. There was no difficulty in finding it, navigating by nose. They towed it to the pier, where a mat was floated underneath, and the body gently lifted by crane.

The river surrendered Flight Sergeant Greener at Brough Haven on Tuesday, 30 August, and the Senior Naval Officer asked whether the Conservancy Board might 'kindly arrange to bring the body to Hull'. In consultation with Supt. Huddleston of the Brough Police, it was decided that 'legal difficulties' (unspecified, but possibly to do with keeping all Coroner's work in one parish) could be avoided if the Board's launch could collect the body. The *W. S. Wright* was duly dispatched to Brough bearing several Americans and Mr Robinson, Undertaker, of Hessle Road, and an undertaker's shell. At 4pm the Hull Police took delivery at Victoria Pier. Next to surface was Chief Machinist's Mate Welch, USN, exactly one week after the disaster, and still wearing a diamond ring - to the surprise (and credit) of the crew of *Hikibydo* who found him. The *Pilot* launch was busy again on Friday and Saturday, conveying '6 officers of the U.S.A. Air Force (sic)' to Immingham to fetch a body, and finding another unnamed victim in Hull Roads.

Eventually the Americans recovered all of their sixteen colleagues, who were shipped back to the United States for burial. Two embalmers who had been preparing American war dead for repatriation were imported from France to supplement the local facilities, this service being something of a luxury in Yorkshire. The weather being fine and premises overcrowded, young George Nicholson and his friends were able to peer over a fence in fascinated horror as the experts worked in an undertaker's open yard.

As the salvage efforts continued, Mr Secretary Franklin was

Fig. 74 The instrument panel from the control car, with the clock stopped five minutes after the accident.

Fig. 75 Tangled wreckage on the stern of a tug awaits transfer to Riverside Quay.

Fig. 76 Trapped in the wreckage, a drowned crewman is discovered during the salvage operation.

Fig. 77 A victim is handed to the police at Victoria Pier.

obliged to issue a supplementary *Notice to Mariners*, requesting vessels to give the wreckage a wider berth. Presumably reflecting the growing dispute over ownership (and liability) it was headed *Airship R.38*, not *ZR-2*.

XVI

To Express an Opinion

Before the shock and grief had given way to guilt and recriminations, and even before the dead could be suitably honoured, there was the inevitable service ritual of the Court of Inquiry. It was convened 'by Command of the Air Council' at RAF Airship Base, Howden, at 10:00 hours on Saturday 27 August 1921. It was to 'enquire into the circumstances occasioning the loss of H.M.A. R.38 on August 24th 1921, and to express an opinion as to the possible causes of the loss.' It followed the time-honoured naval practice of determining responsibility for the loss of a ship, but perhaps in deference to the prominence of the major casualties the customary instruction 'to apportion blame if any' was not used. It may also have been omitted by an Air Council which already had pangs of guilt over the shortening of the air tests.

Although the inquiry was to be followed by a technical review by the Accidents Investigation Sub-Committee of the new Aeronautical Research Committee, it was essential to establish the sequence of events while the evidence was still fresh and unclouded by too much retelling or revision.

The membership of the Court was impressive, reflecting the seriousness of the loss in terms of prestige, cost, implications for aviation and also the political and international ramifications. With Air Vice Marshal (later Marshal of the Royal Air Force) Sir John Salmond as President, the seven other members included Group Captain (later Air Chief Marshal) Sir Arthur Longmore and Squadron Leader R. B. B. Colmore (who was to die, as Director of Airship Development, in R.101 in 1930). The talented Wing Commander Cave-Brown-Cave was balanced by the anti-airship Air Commodore Scarlett, who had attempted to prove the worthlessness of blimps at Mudros in 1915. As C I. R. Campbell was dead, the Royal Corps of Naval Constructors (begetters of R.38) were represented by A. W. Johns, Esq. The impressively tall Commander Horace T. Dyer was present as an observer on behalf of the United States Navy.

The first witness to be called was Air Vice Marshal A. V. Vyvyan, who in the course of five answers totalling thirty words was able to wash his hands of the proceedings. He was followed by Messrs. May, Gerrish and Evans of the Royal Airship Works, who bore the brunt of the questioning relating to the construction and trials; the hapless Henry May suffering two whole days of inquisition, with supplementary recalls.

This was followed by evidence from eye witnesses and survivors, of which Harry Bateman's was the most accurate, detailed and dramatic. RAF and USN crewmen who had been on previous trials were also called to comment on the control problems which had been experienced.

Finally the RAW personnel were again questioned about the weaknesses detected during the building and the first three flights.

As the transcript of the Inquiry has already been used in reconstructing the story, it would be tedious to quote from it at length. However, it did draw certain conclusions, and in the light of later research and of opinions given to the author by other airship historians, it is necessary to recount some of the proceedings.

Having established the sequence of tests, trials and attendant misfortunes during construction and early flights, the Court proceeded to Hull on Tuesday, 30 August 'to inspect the scene of the accident and the salved parts of the Airship'. Mr. May was again on hand to explain that the recovered girders showed an initial break between Frames 9 and 10 and a second separation between Frames 4 and 5. Traces of fire were only evident in the keel, but three petrol tanks which had been recovered had definitely exploded.

The Court then took itself to London, where it reassembled at 10:30 hours on Wednesday to examine the written evidence and summon witnesses in the greater comfort and convenience of the Air Ministry.

That night, at midnight, almost unnoticed by court or country, the Great War was officially ended by the ratification of the Peace Treaty. Its main effect was the replacement of D.O.R.A. (the Defence of the Realm Act) by new licensing regulations, thus perpetuating the wartime restrictions on public house opening hours.

Back in Yorkshire, where the Humber was soon to yield an almost daily quota of bodies, a Coroner's Jury had been sworn in by Dr T. C. Jackson (acting Coroner of Kingston upon Hull) at Hull Royal Infirmary, where they were shown the body of the 'dead on arrival' Lieutenant C. G. Little, USN, laid out by the meticulous Head Porter, Mr Harry Grainger. From here they were conducted to view the remains of Flight Lieutenant Montagu, RAF, and Lieutenant Marcus H. Esterley, USN, whose prudent emergency radio had been as impotent in the circumstances as his 'lucky bone of a churchyard rabbit'. In anticipation of a number of visitors, some attempt had been made to soften the horror.

BEAUTIFUL FLOWERS AT THE MORTUARY

> Arrangements have been made at the Castle Street mortuary for the reception of a large number of dead. The sombre chamber has been beautified by flowers, and the remains of the self-sacrificing airmen will be treated with tenderness and devotion.

The formal opening of the inquest at the Guildhall gave some sense of dignity to the otherwise sordid activity and it was honoured by the presence of Air Vice Marshal Vyvyan and the Revd D. L. Viener, Chaplain-in-Chief of the RAF, as well as Mr J. Grout, American Consul at Hull, with some of the USN officers of the Howden Detachment. Also present were the parents of Flight Lieutenant Montagu, to hear Dr Jackson address a message of sympathy 'to the sorrowing relatives of the deceased men, whether they be citizens of this Empire or our sister nation'. He then adjourned the inquest (subject to the need for further certificates for interment) until 4 October, when it was hoped that Flight Lieutenant Wann would be sufficiently recovered to give evidence.

At the Air Ministry the Court of Inquiry continued the delicate task of sifting evidence which, though given in good faith, often differed in detail or in substance, and reflected the subjectivity of the shocked witnesses. There were conflicting reports of the number of parachutes which had descended, in spite of the thousands of citizens who were watching; but as no parachutist survived, the question was academic. Some bodies were reported to be wearing harness and there had been parachutes for all, but the blazing fuel would have disposed of any open canopies. The fragments of silk which still exist as souvenirs suggest that some 'chutes were opened. Ironically, Harry Bateman probably escaped a fiery death by failing to jump clear.

The timing, sequence and location of the fire were also the subjects of confused observation. At least one witness was convinced that both halves had burned, in spite of the safe descent of the after portion. Estimates of the delay between the fire and the explosions varied from five to thirty seconds. It was concluded that the breakage had simultaneously broken a petrol line and an electric circuit and that a spark had started the fire which in turn had detonated hydrogen from ruptured gas cells.

The sceptical and now smug Mr Cann, who had predicted that the ship would not reach America, offered evidence but perhaps happily did not receive his summons in time to attend, although his letter was submitted to the Court. Other theorists, not called to appear, offered their views to a willing press in which the arguments persisted for some weeks alongside the reports of disturbances in Ireland and Germany and the Fatty Arbuckle murder trial in America.

Having more or less established the sequence and the probable immediate causes of the accident, the Court addressed the delicate matter of personal responsibility, both for the design and construction and in the conduct of the flight trials.

It was acknowledged that the *wartime* requirements had been 'greatly in advance of those of previous British airships' and that they had imposed 'the utmost economy in hull weights and materials'. There were many new design features, in spite of 'a lack of vital aerodynamical information as to the effect of these modifications on the strength of the structure'. However, they pointed out that after the Armistice it should have been possible to use information regarding airships built elsewhere - presumably a reference to Pritchard's *Zeppelin* reports. (The subsequent technical inquiry turned up a list of reports which should have been available to Campbell, if he had had time to read them.)

The overloading of Campbell was tacitly recognised by the criticism that 'the construction of the ship and the inspection work . . . centred in one head' was unsound, and that the 'design should have been examined and discussed by an official and competent Committee before the actual construction was commenced'. This seemingly realistic appraisal and sensible suggestion was included in the document signed at the Air Ministry, London, on 5 September 1921. The same Air Ministry had just excluded Vickers, employers of the two most experienced airship designers in the country (Pratt and Wallis), from any further airship work! Incredibly, the same 'centring in one head' was to be repeated in the building of R.101, when the Royal Airship Works declined any consultation with Barnes Wallis and the Vickers team who were building the rival R.100.

* * *

If the initial Inquiry raised more questions than it answered it at least expedited the setting up of the Aeronautical Research Committee, comprising a good mix of established scientists and experienced aeronauts. Its Chairman was Lieutenant Colonel Mervyn O'Gorman, who had been Superintendent of Farnborough from 1909 to 1916 and was a member of the Advisory Committee for

Aeronautics, founded in 1909. O'Gorman had notable airship experience, having accompanied Murray Sueter (the pair of them disguised as Americans) on their clandestine tour of French, German and Austrian airship facilities in 1912. The light-hearted espionage included a five and a half hour flight in the DELAG Zeppelin, *Viktoria Luise*. Major Scott and Wing Commander Cave-Brown-Cave represented the practising airshipmen, and they were complemented by academic scientists such as Professors Bairstow, CBE, FRS, and Sutton Pippard, AMInstCE, FRAeS, with a team which was capable of doing all the sums required in a highly technical investigation.

During the next four months, in the course of eighteen meetings and considerable homework, they did all the checking of calculations which should have *preceded* the actual building of the ship. They took the time to read twenty-nine research papers relating to aerodynamic forces on actual airships or models. Ten of these, including pioneering work by M. Eiffel of Tower fame, had been published before the first two frames of R.38 had been joined. In five of the reports, Campbell is listed as co-author with Pannell of the NPL!

To their amazement, they discovered that *no allowance* had been made for *aerodynamic* stresses in the design, which was based on static load/buoyancy conditions in level flight. There was thus no reserve strength to cope with the unknown forces. In engineering terms, the *factor of safety of 4* for the static condition reduced to *1* when likely air pressures were taken into account. The structure was virtually condemned to fail at first overload.

The Committee concluded that during the final flight 'no loads were imposed in excess of those which might have occurred during the normal navigation of the ship in weather which might reasonably be encountered'; but that 'owing to the instability of the airship, the movements of the controls necessary to keep her on any particular course were large and rapid'. This in their opinion, was the straw which broke the back of the structure 'not improbably weakened by the cumulative effects of reversals of stress' accentuated by the 'specially powerful control surfaces of new design', i.e. the still overly-balanced rudders and elevators.

It was not in the brief of this Committee to apportion blame, only to establish causes and to recommend safeguards. Campbell was dead and unable to defend himself, but he was certainly not responsible for the specification handed to him in 1918 for the design of a super naval airship. His culpability, if any, was in failing even to guess at aerodynamic effects, or to ask for a revised performance requirement when the fighting ended. A concluding paragraph in the Committee's report perhaps hints at this personal failing:

Fig. 78 Wing Commander T R Cave-Brown-Cave CBE was a leading airship expert from 1913 to 1931. Co-designer of the *Submarine Scout* blimp and its successors, he later specialised in engines. He was a key member of the Courts of Inquiry into the R.38/ZR-2 disaster. Photo: Yorkshire Air Museum

Fig. 79 Mr William Joy being interviewed by Geoff Drewitt for Anglia Television in 1970. Bill Joy worked at the Airship Station before and after War service in the Tank Corps. During the building of R.100 (1926-29) he was chauffeur to the Airship Guarantee Company.

That on the assumptions made, the structure was designed with great skill and the necessary calculations were carefully carried out by methods admitted as sufficiently accurate in *other branches* of engineering practice.

The italics are mine. C. I. R. Campbell was a former designer of submarines.

On the cause of the fire, the Accidents Investigation Sub-Committee merely endorsed the opinion of the court of Inquiry that simultaneous fractures of petrol pipes and electric circuits were to blame. Some subsequent research cast doubt on this, but without supplying an alternative theory. It is my opinion, following discussions with aviation historians and a former British Aerospace researcher, that vaporised petrol was indeed ignited by sparks from a broken cable. To avoid boring the general reader, this theory and further thoughts about the mechanics of the breakup of the hull framework will be found in Appendix A.

* * *

So what did go wrong, and who was to blame?

Disregarding the errors in design, which were due to too little research and too much innovation, there is the question of why a ship designed as a *height climber* should have been deliberately stressed at a *low altitude*. It was the folly of Icarus, albeit in reverse.

We have seen how the cautious and highly qualified J. E. M. Pritchard had been forced to modify his progressive test programme from 150 hours to 50 hours. Even shortly before the final flight he was reminding his superiors that the tests should be carried out above 7,500 feet, following Zeppelin practice. How then could he have decided - or have been persuaded - on the apparently reckless manoeuvring at low altitude? It is unlikely that he was overruled by Maitland or overawed by Maxfield, both of whom respected his experience and judgement. Considering the number of experienced airshipmen and scientists on board, it can only have been a consensus decision involving Maitland, Maxfield, Pannell, Wann and probably I. C. Little, arrived at in the Control Car after the high-speed run. Icarus was a committee!

It cannot have been an easy decision, as the risks were known, and we can only guess that they were weighed against other factors, chiefly the need to pronounce the airship airworthy enough to cross the Atlantic. The rough weather tests had not yet been possible, but time was running out. In a few days at the most, ZR-2 would be preparing to depart from the Pulham mast for America. In the absence of rough air, severe control movements in dense air would have to simulate storm stresses. (Major Scott, who had taken R.34 to America and back, agreed in evidence that the stresses would be similar.)

The decision taken, the crew members were ordered once more to watch stations (though not all obeyed) and the speed was worked up to 54 knots.

It is reasonable to ask why such a dangerous evolution should have been taken near a large city and not over the North Sea. The only reasonable answer is that it was the last chance to complete the tasks before returning to Howden (with an exhausted and hungry crew) where a large party of soldiers and airmen was waiting to land and house the ship. The Humber was in sight ahead, and its wide waters would lead all the way back to base. If some girders should fail (as on previous trips) would it not be preferable to be within reasonable distance of a landing ground with repair facilities than over an unfriendly ocean? They may also have been reassured by the good behaviour of the ship up to this point in the final flight, notably the lack of damage to the vulnerable control surfaces following the high speed run, when Campbell and Maitland had come aft to speak to Bateman at his lonely station.

In the event, ZR-2 had cleared the land on an apparently safe course before anything broke. Ironically, the newspaper reports that Captain Wann had saved Hull by skilful steering was far from the truth, as he later testified. The stricken ship, breaking first on one side and bending like a boomerang, veered out of control in an arc towards the crowded centre of Hull and the terrified watchers on the waterfront. Mercifully for thousands it fell in the water just short of Victoria Pier.

We are left with the impression that a handful of professionally competent and brave men took a calculated risk to prevent a later disaster over the Atlantic. To those who like to apportion blame (always legion after a catastrophe) it may have seemed reckless. They might like to consider the possible recklessness of Treasury, Air Ministry and US Navy Department officials and their political masters, who cynically overrode the advice of the experts in order to expedite the sale of R.38/ZR-2.

XVII

La mer son sépulture

Of all the formal, official expressions of grief the memorial service on Wednesday 31 August in St. Peter's Church, Howden, was probably the most moving and heartfelt. A town which had identified itself with the life of the airship base could not fail to share the sense of loss of its guest airmen and the pain of their families, a number of whom had lodged in the town. Some had been married in the ancient Minster church. Four hundred RAF men and the remaining members of the USN Howden Detachment, led by Lieutenant R. G. Pennoyer, took their reserved places before the townspeople (who had closed all shops and businesses) crowded into the church. Relatives and friends of some of the victims were present. The band of the Royal Inniskilling Dragoons from the York Garrison, which customarily provided airship handling parties, was in the chancel to play 'Ave Maria' and 'O Rest in the Lord' (Mendelsson).

This was a local community mourning its dead. The service was taken by Squadron Leader the Revd W. T. Rees, Chaplain of Howden RAF Station, assisted by the Revd A. Waring, Vicar of Howden, and the Revd Kellett (curate). The Revd S. J. Soadby, Vicar of Elloughton, represented the church where four of the American officers had worshipped and where a tablet would later be placed to their memory. The simple and sincere service closed with the playing of Chopin's Funeral March.

On the following day the City of Kingston upon Hull honoured the fallen in a memorial service in Holy Trinity Church, attended by the robed civic dignitaries, members of the armed forces and as many of the public as could be admitted. Ex-servicemen were particularly asked to attend. Such was the crush that many were turned away and the musical parts of the service were repeated on the following Sunday evening for those still wishing to pay their respects in church.

Friday 2 September was the day for the first of the funerals. Five victims, including Mr C. W. Duffield of the National Physical Laboratory, had already been dispatched by rail for burial at their homes, but a grave plot had been reserved in the Hull Western Cemetery for those whose families would prefer a service burial. The first five to share the communal grave were Air Commodore Maitland, Flight Lieutenants I. C. Little and R. S. Montagu, Constructor Commander Campbell and Leading Aircraftman J. W. Wilson. The democratic, gregarious Edward Maitland would certainly have approved of this final abandonment of rank, but full military honours were accorded on the way, with Air Marshall Sir H. M. Trenchard, Bart, KCB, DSO, representing the King and the Air Council. Senior members of all services were present, together with Sir Frederick Sykes, Controller in Chief of Civil Aviation and Lieutenant Commander R. E. Byrd for the US Naval Bureau of Aeronautics. The officers and men of the Howden Detachment were again in attendance.

It was an impressive occasion, organised by a young but proud Royal Air Force which, in the process of post-war running down, had suddenly become exceedingly newsworthy. It now showed what it could do in the way of ceremonial when required.

From early morning of Friday 2 September the grounds of the City Mortuary had been filling up with flowers from many organisations and individuals, while the more personal tributes were placed inside the building or on the plain coffins. Some of the accompanying inscriptions provided good journalistic copy, such as a wreath of 'a broken heart of white lilies and asters, with pink carnations just where the severance occurred', with a card in a lady's hand 'To Air Commodore Maitland. A heart from the heart of your dearest friend - Lily Charlesworth.' Another read 'Oh! great brave friend of England, in England's heart you will live for ever.' On the evidence of the number of wreaths dedicated to him by friends and comrades, past and present, as well as formal and official tributes, Edward Maitland would live in many hearts.

No less sincere were the expressions of sympathy from other RAF stations, and from individuals and organisations without connections with aviation. The residents of some streets had combined to send flowers, and the Holy Trinity Day Schools offered 'a token of sympathy and condolence for the safety of Old Town.' A wreath of red roses, white and blue chrysanthemums and white lilies was 'In loving memory of the RAF Heroes from their American Comrades.' Even the crew of the 80-ton crane, still probing the wreckage for the missing, were represented by a floral tribute.

In the early afternoon the coffins were placed on two aircraft trailers, draped with Union flags and covered by wreaths. The motor

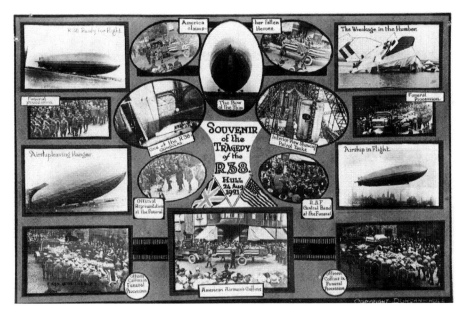

Fig. 80 A montage postcard of photographs relating to the career of R.38, from building to disaster, and including the funerals.

Fig. 81 R.38/ZR-2 superimposed photographically on the Hull skyline by a postcard publisher.

In Memory

of the

Officers and Men who perished in the

R 38,

on Wednesday, August 24th,

1921.

BRITISH OFFICERS.

Air Commodore E. M. Maitland, C.M.G., D.S.O., A.F.C.
Flight-Lieut. G. N. Thomas, D.F.C.
Flight-Lieut. I. C. Little.
Flight-Lieut. R. F. Montagu, D.F.C.

Flying Officer V. H. Wicks.
Flying Officer P. F. Mathewson, A.F.C.
Flt.-Lt. J. E. M. Pritchard, O.B.E., A.F.C.
Mr. C. J. R. Campbell, Supt. Rl. A. W.
Mr. F. Warrenn, Royal Airship Works.

BRITISH OTHER RANKS.

Flight-Sergts. F. J. Heath, W. H. Greenel, H. Tompson, F. Smith, J. Rye, and A. P. Martin.   A.C.I. C. W. Penson, Sergt. J. W. Mason, Sergt. F. W. Burton, L.A.C. G. S. Anger, A.C.I. J. C. Drew, A.C.I. C. W. Donald, W. Oliver, R. Parker, E. E. Speere, J. M. Wilson, R. Withington.

AMERICAN OFFICERS.

Comdr. L. A. H. Maxfield, U.S.N.
Lieut.-Comdr. W. N. Bieg, U.S.N.
Lieut.-Comdr. G. W. Coel, U.S.N.

Lieut. H. W. Hoyt, U.S.N.
Lieut.-Comdr. G. G. Little, U.S.N.
Lieut. M. M. Esterly, U.S.N.

AMERICANS (OTHER NAVAL RANKS).

C.M.M. L. E. Crowl, C.M.M. A. L. Loftin, C.M.M. P. Julino, C.M.M. G. Welsh, C.B.M. C. J. Aller, C.M.M. J. T. Hancock, C.B.M. B. M. Lay, C.M.M. R. M. Coons, C.M.M. W. J. Steele, C.B.M. A. D. Pittitt.

Fig. 82 The memorial card, hurriedly printed for the service in Holy Trinity Church, contains many spelling errors.

Fig. 83 The first funeral cortege passes through Victoria Square.

Fig. 84 The sixteen American casualties commence their journey home from the old Hull Royal Infirmary in Prospect Street.

Fig. 85 The memorial in Hull Western Cemetery in 1970.
The missing centre plaque has since been replaced. An unknown hand still places
occasional flowers on the plinth.

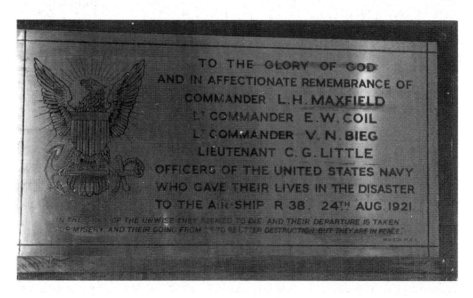

Fig. 86 The memorial plaque in Elloughton Church.

Fig. 87 Memorial in the London Headquarters of the Royal Aeronautical Society.

tenders which pulled the trailers were also loaded with flowers. At three o'clock the procession set out, led by the firing party of 100 men from Howden under their new Commanding Officer, Wing Commander Cunningham. In slow time, with arms reversed, they preceded the Central Band of the Royal Air Force. Next came the motor tenders and trailers, flanked by the escort party and the pall bearers, including four officers of the United States Navy. Following, mostly on foot, came the personal mourners and then the long procession of official representatives of the services and government departments.

At 4pm the large crowd around the roped enclosure at the cemetery, many of whom had already waited for several hours, heard Chopin's Funeral March and the measured tramp of the procession along Spring Bank, but it was another fifteen minutes before the cortège arrived and a further delay before the coffins, flowers and mourners were in place.

The brief and formal ritual of the committal, conducted by the Chaplain-in-Chief of the RAF and the Chaplain of Howden Airship Station, was concluded by three volleys fired over the grave and the sounding of the Last Post. Then having placed the huge mound of flowers over and around the grave, the servicemen withdrew, to be replaced by the less dignified and jostling crowd.

While recognising that there is an undeniable fascination in tragedy, it is reasonable to speculate that many who packed City Square that day, or who lined the two mile route to the Western Cemetery, or waited hours at the graveside, may have found an element of catharsis for personal grief in the pageantry. Hull had contributed its quota to the dead and missing on land and sea in the Great War - so recently ended - and it is not unlikely that the dignified and moving formality of the occasion was to many spectators a 'funeral by proxy' for their own loved ones - just as the national honouring of an Unknown Warrior provides a focus for mourning for those who have no known grave.

Four days later, with military and civil honours, and attended by widows and friends, a cortege of coffins draped with the Stars and Stripes left the mortuary of Hull Royal Infirmary in Prospect Street for Paragon Station, where they were entrained for Devonport. Here they were embarked on *HMS Dauntless* for the voyage to Brooklyn Navy Yard. Somewhere in the Atlantic the engines were stopped for the burial at sea of Lieutenant Commander Coil, in accordance with his wish. On Friday 16 September *Dauntless's* sailors and Royal Marines handed the fifteen coffins to their trans-Atlantic colleagues for a dockside service, after which most were consigned to their home towns, American style, for interment with naval honours. Three were laid to rest in the huge National Cemetery at Arlington,

Virginia. They were Commander Maxfield, Lieutenant Commander Bieg and Chief Machinist's Mate Welch. Chief Bosun's Mate Charles Aller, whose timely phone call from Frame 7 during the third flight had possibly postponed the end, rests in the Fort Rosecrans National Cemetery at San Diego.

Back in Britain, the national homage had been paid in Westminster Abbey on Wednesday 7 September by a distinguished and international congregation which included the United States Ambassador and Chancellor and representatives of the King, Queen Alexandra the Queen Mother and the Duke of York. Among the glittering company of service and civic dignitaries, the relatively humble mourners were shown to their reserved places. Caught arriving with two of her children by the *Daily Mirror* photographer, Mrs Pritchard was wrongly reported as the widow of an American. This trivial journalistic error - possibly due to her husband's American parentage - can only have added to her sense of loss. With five others, the talented the honourable John Edward Maddock Pritchard was to remain among the missing.

The River Humber having ceased to deliver up the dead, the last four bodies were borne to the Western Cemetery on 8 September. With no less reverence but an inevitable sense of anticlimax, Flying Officer Matthewson, Flight Sergeant Rye, Leading Aircraftman Oliver and Assistant Constructor Warren joined their comrades.

In April 1924 a memorial in Portland stone designed by Major Winton Newman, FRIBA, and executed by Mr Wrigglesworth of Hull was unveiled at the grave by Air Vice Marshall Sir Vyell Vyvyan and dedicated by the Bishop of Hull. Among the company were Wann, Bateman and Potter. The United States was represented by Captain Hussey, US Naval Attaché. Two bronze plaques recorded the names of the 28 British and 16 American casualties. A third bronze with a dedication subsequently went missing, apparently stolen, but has since been replaced by a stone tablet. From time to time an unknown hand places a small vase of flowers on the plinth.

In the rural peace of Elloughton Church, a memorial plaque is dedicated to Commander Maxfield, Lieutenant Commanders Coil and Bieg and Lieutenant Little, USN, close to the Humberside village of Brough where they lodged while on the Howden Detachment.

The Royal Aeronautical Society also launched a memorial fund, but with the practical idea of investing the capital and using the income to investigate problems 'connected with airships or allied subjects'. The research would be stimulated by an annual competition for the best technical paper on aeronautics, to be open to international competition. The prize of 25 guineas (£26.25) - no mean sum at the time - was probably less important than the honour of being chosen to present the paper. This economical incentive ensured that the Society could also commission a memorial tablet for its London headquarters, from John Paul Cooper, Sculptor:

> In memory of those who died
> in H. M. Airship R38
> which failed and fell
> 24th August 1921

Under the crests of the Royal Air Force, the United States Navy, the Royal Corps of Naval Constructors and the National Physical Laboratory are the names of the victims. Above is a suspended model of the airship.

The memorial competition continues to this day.

If all this ceremonial seems disproportionate, it should be remembered that the loss was greater and more complicated than the death of 44 brave men. At the time of great expectations for the new Air Age, when passenger aeroplanes were still small, uncomfortable and limited in range, the giant dirigible seemed to promise an elegant and glamorous alternative. For many, it was a symbol of the Brave New World, a weapon of war with great potential for peaceful use. It would build bridges, speed communications with the Empire and friendly nations. Britain had built the state-of-the-art airship, and the country was proud that our great new ally wanted it. (Most people were not to know that the sale represented an abandonment of our interest for cash - a not uncommon British failing.) In the circumstances, the R.38/ZR-2 tragedy was an immense blow to national pride and confidence, akin to the loss of the *Titanic*.

* * *

While the expressions of sympathy were still being exchanged, the accountants were at work to decide who was to pay for what. Officially, the ship had not been accepted by the United States at the time of the accident and was under British command, although jointly crewed. After much argument, the two nations agreed to split the loss at around $1,000,000 (£250,000 approx) each. Nevertheless the Americans were billed for £156 in respect of deficiencies and barrack damages at Howden!

On 20 October the Air Ministry wrote that 'it was not the wish of the Air Council' that the Humber Conservancy Board should undertake any further salvage work at their expense, but they would still like to examine any wreckage found. In reply, Secretary Franklin quoted the Humber Conservancy Act (1899) by which he was obliged to remove any wreckage which might be a hazard to navigation at the cost of the owner. Possibly feeling that the Air Ministry's attitude was less than generous, in view of all the help given by the City, the Hull Corporation Property Committee added its own claim for damages of £108 2s. 8d. (£108.13) to the many already received by the Air Ministry.

The salvage operation was formally ended on 7 November, when it was reported that the channel had been repeatedly swept and was now clear for navigation. Parts of the tail section on the Middle Sand would be reduced to sand level and abandoned.

Tenders were invited for the salvaged material, which was bought by the Tooley and Fenton foundry of Hull, to be turned into candlesticks and ashtrays for Hull Brewery. Other portions which came into private hands were kept as souvenirs or processed into ornaments. Some of the girders were tested for fatigue or fire damage, and it was probably from this stock that B. N. Wallis of Vickers made a charm pendant for eleven year old Edna Wilson, the sister of a colleague.

Perhaps some day the restless currents of the Humber will deliver up some of the estimated one per cent of the great airship which lies buried in the sand.

XVIII

A Phoenix or two

As soon as it seemed decently safe to do so, the detractors emerged to harass the supporters of lighter-than-air flight. Their motives ranged from economy to timidity and from vested interest to plain carping of the 'I told you so' variety. Some of the criticism had merit and might have profited later planners if the bitterness of the attacks had not merely polarised and hardened attitudes.

Also, while the Court of Inquiry had glossed over the issue of personal culpability, there were moves by the Air Ministry to fix the blame for faulty design on the Admiralty whose Royal Corps of Naval Constructors had in fact designed R.38. The Admiralty responded that although the design was 'in advance of anything hitherto attempted, it did not incorporate any novel features which would affect the strength and safety of the ship, and that no undue risk was taken in the design.' This was at odds with the Air Ministry contention that the 'new requirements were far ahead of anything previously demanded of British airships' - a justifiable reference to the all-embracing specification drawn up by the Admiralty. The Air Ministry might have been tempted to add that no undue care had been taken to consider the aerodynamic forces, as the Accidents Investigation Sub-Committee clearly blamed faulty design and not manoeuvres outside the scope of the tests.

The arguments between departments, in Parliament, and in the aeronautical press rumbled on for several years until they were overtaken by the controversy surrounding the Burney Imperial Airship Scheme. The accident had come at a bad time for the lighter-than-air lobby, as a conference of Imperial Prime Ministers had been discussing air services during the previous month, and had even enjoyed a flight in R.33 from Croydon to Pulham on 16 July, (although one wonders how they enjoyed the vertical ladder descent from the liftless Pulham mast!).

Commander Dennistoun (later Sir Dennis) Burney was the inventor of the *paravane* for cutting the cables of sea mines, and with his royalties he was free to apply his restless energy and inventive mind as he chose. Though no airshipman, he set out to champion the cause of Imperial air communications, for which only the airship possessed both the range and the payload at that time. The scheme which he finally negotiated was basically commercial, sponsored by Vickers and Shell Petroleum and guaranteed by the governments concerned. As the £4M. capital was to be raised by a share issue the British Government could pretend that it was not spending any money, but at the same time satisfying Admiralty and Air Ministry demands for the development of airships with military potential.

By a process of prolonged commercial and political wheeling and dealing, the clever and ambitious Sir Dennis liberated the Phoenix of the big rigid dirigible from the ashes of disaster.

In the event he raised a double-headed Phoenix because the 1924 General Election returned a Labour Government which did not like the commercial basis of the Burney Scheme and saw a promising opening for State enterprise.

After much wrangling, a truly British compromise commissioned one ship from Vickers and reactivated the Royal Airship Works, Cardington, to build a rival. They were soon dubbed the Capitalist Ship and the Socialist Ship by the press.

For many former airship people this was good news, but it posed a problem for the two teams who were competing for the available design staff, labour and building berths. The Cardington shed, with modifications, could accommodate the state-built R.101, while one of the two Pulham sheds would be transferred and enlarged to house the rival R.100 when built. Vickers, who did not have a large enough shed at Barrow, bought the surviving double shed at Howden in the name of its subsidiary, the Airship Guarantee Company, thus giving the old town echoes of its former glory and the prospect of some employment.

To those who look for the hand of Fortune in events, the slender-won, tentative decision to revive the airship programme and the resulting recall of Mr B. N. Wallis as Chief Designer of R.100 must have a special significance. He had been designing the Vickers Zeppelin-type airships to Admiralty specifications since 1913 and had been involved in many experiments with light alloys and with mooring towers. He had designed R.80, the small, streamlined and highly efficient rigid airship for Fleet operations which was completed too late for war service but which helped to train the Howden Detachment. With the attenuation of the airship service he had put in his time on a meagre retainer until dismissed early in 1922, and had since been teaching in a public school in Switzerland.

His beautiful R.80 had been retired and was about to be dismantled. Now, with a virtually free hand, he was to show his amazing capacity for innovation in a structure completely unlike any previous airship. In the shed where R.38/ZR-2 had nursed her conventional Zeppelin-type broken ribs, he fabricated a unique web of helically-wound tubes into a hull half as big again as any previous British dirigible. This airframe would never buckle and break.

Although some key personnel had served at Barrow, the bulk of the labour force was recruited locally and from the ports of the Humber.

Howden was once more an airship town, and proud of it.

It was the designing of a novel system of gas bag retaining wires, distributing the lift evenly to the hull, that inspired the *geodetic* construction later used in the series of Wallis-designed bombers - most notably the *Wellington* - which in turn gave him the status and the power-base to develop his dam-busting and earthquake bombs and to pursue his researches into high speed flight and many other projects.

But to return to Howden. On a misty December morning in 1929, R.100 was walked from the huge shed and released for transfer to Cardington and a series of tests which culminated in a triumphant flight to Canada. The proud men and women who had built her were laid off, but with the expectation of further orders when the Imperial Airship Scheme got underway.

R.101, dogged by development problems, overweight due to the use of diesel engines and a very robust frame (both inspired by the memory of R.38), was hurried through its tests and to its fiery end on a French hillside in the early hours of 5 October 1930. Nothing, apparently, had been learned about the hazards of political control of scientific development.

Among the casualties was Flight Sergeant Walter Potter, Assistant Coxswain, who had not even got wet on 21 August 1921.

It was also the end for R.100, which was scrapped in spite of its successful record, thus terminating Britain's brief encounter with the giant rigid airship.

* * *

What of the other survivors of R.38/ZR-2? Flight Lieutenant Archie Wann recovered from his physical injuries and remained in the RAF, although he was back in hospital from time to time. The author's father, recovering from the trauma of a Bristol Fighter crash, encountered him in an RAF hospital at Finchley some time after the R.38 incident. In 1930 he flew as a supernumerary officer on R.100's Canadian flight, with the rank of Squadron Leader. He must have had a bad moment when a squall tore large sections of the fabric from the fins over the St. Lawrence River (reminiscent of the Humber?) and he accompanied First Officer George Meager and Chief Calculator Nevil Shute Norway to inspect the damage.

At St. Hubert's Airport, Montreal, he had the less harrowing task of arranging visits to the airship's accommodation. Either at his own request or to avoid spoiling the promotional aspect of the visit, his previous unhappy airship experience received no publicity.

He was not on the return flight to Cardington having been given charge of the 'spare watch' which travelled by sea, their places taken by the advance party which had been sent over to await R.100's arrival in Canada.

Shortly afterwards he had a harrowing appointment as Registrar to the Court of Inquiry into the R.101 disaster in which so many more of his contemporaries had died. With the scarcity of experienced airship captains he was the obvious choice, but it must have rekindled some unpleasant memories.

With the abandonment of airships in Britain he was sent to the RAF Staff College and then in 1932 to Calshot to train as a flying boat pilot. During the 1939-45 war he was for some time AOC (Air Officer Commanding) in Malta before being posted to the Air Ministry for work in connection with Morale and Rehabilitation, for which he would seem to have been uniquely qualified by experience.

He retired in 1946 with the rank of Air Commodore and died in the South of France on 11 October 1948 at the age of 53.

* * *

Harry Bateman, who had survived by the fortunate, if a trifle ignominious, tangling of his parachute went on to a distinguished scientific career in aviation and guided weapons development. Apparently unharmed by his ordeal, he gave valuable evidence to the accident investigations and returned to work on wind tunnel evaluation of aircraft wings and propellers; but nature imposed a strange penance for his survival and he lost all his hair, which was not restored to him for two years.

Alternating between Teddington, Farnborough and Cardington he worked on projects as diverse as balloon design and rocket propulsion. He was involved in work on both R.100 and R.101 and in the design of air/sea rescue dinghies and high altitude barrage balloons.

One afternoon during World War II he was called in by Churchill, along with other 'boffins', to submit ideas by next morning 'to annoy Hitler cheaply.' He devised an 8 feet diameter balloon fitted with an alarm clock mechanism which could be launched towards Germany on a favouring wind. On its pre-set E.T.A. it would release either a fine wire to short-circuit overhead electricity cables, or a sunlight-activated incendiary paper to cause multiple fires in forests. It is not known whether these particular dirty tricks were ever employed.

A more spectacular wartime assignment was in the evaluation of solid rockets and firing mechanisms at Farnborough, where a vehicle known as the 'flaming hearse' would thunder and belch along a rail track to the alarm of visitors.

In August 1943 he was sufficiently regarded professionally to be flown to the Quebec Conference in the bomb bay of a *Liberator*. This was the major meeting at which Roosevelt and Churchill agreed on the development of the atomic bomb and nuclear energy, and the Combined Chiefs of Staff discussed the future conduct of the war.

In 1945 he became Superintendent of the Balloon Development Establishment, renamed Cardington Research and Development Establishment; in effect the post once held by C. I. R. Campbell.

His work with rockets led to his appointment as Assistant Director Controlled Projectiles (U.K.) and in this capacity he was involved in the launching experiments at Woomera, Australia.

In 1945 he was awarded the OBE.

His active contribution to science did not cease with his retirement in 1959, as he employed his didactic and mathematical skills in teaching students who showed promise but were handicapped by a weakness in maths.

During the 1930s the BBC made a series of magazine programmes, each dealing with a specific year. In 1935 Harry Bateman recounted his R.38 ordeal in *Scrapbook for 1921*, which was in effect the first publication of his story.

Harry Bateman died in Bedford in July 1969 at the age of 72.

* * *

Norman Walker, whose youthful keenness or his guardian angel had directed him to the tail cockpit, remained in the United States Navy until 1923. He was then employed as a civilian at Lakehurst, N.J., which was to have been the home base of ZR-2.

Following the R.101 disaster in 1930, he wrote to Bateman in a reminiscent mood recalling that they had last seen each other in a Hull police cell when they were drying out after the rescue. He was obviously distressed by the death of their co-survivor Walter Potter: 'It seems as tho he was doomed to die in an airship wreck.' Strangely, he did not mention the loss of *Shenandoah* (the US Navy's American-built ZR-1) which had broken up in a line squall in September 1925 with the loss of 14 crew. Instead, as a true airshipman, he expressed his belief in helium, the non-inflammable lifting gas which only the Americans possessed in quantity at that time.

Helium did not save ZR-4, the US Navy's *Akron*, wrecked in the Atlantic in 1933 with the loss of 73 men, or the *Macon*, ZR-5, which fell in the Pacific in 1935 with only two fatalities. It might have saved the *Hindenburg*, whose fiery end at Lakehurst in 1937 is a familiar image on television programmes about airships.

*   *   *

Only one survivor of R.38/ZR-2 is unaccounted for. 239019 Leading Aircraftman Ernest Wynn Davies gave evidence to the Court of Inquiry, but thereafter is not heard nor apparently seen by the press. Perhaps someone who reads this will complete the story.

*   *   *

After any loss, particularly of lives, there is inevitably a reckoning of profit and loss. In R.38/ZR-2 there died some people with considerable potential for the future of aeronautics, and they were not easy to replace. As people they were irreplaceable, but they joined thousands who had gone before (and thousands who would follow) in the pursuit of an ideal.

*   *   *

Some disasters are remembered; others forgotten except by families and friends of the victims, or by eye-witnesses who (in modern terms) have been 'traumatised' by the experience. Perhaps it was only the uniqueness of the timing and setting of this accident which triggered so much public emotion and ensured it a place in most lists of Great Disasters.

With the emotion so far behind us, what can we say about its place in aviation history? What were its achievements, if any? Did its failure teach any useful lessons; if so, were they applied?

Perhaps its greatest legacy was the stimulus which it gave to *research* in aeronautical science, from which the earliest days had been largely by empirical, rule-of thumb methods. Heavier-than-air design had enjoyed the practical feedback from thousands of warplanes and their builders, pilots and ground staff. Wartime aircraft - and men - were expendable. Risks could be taken, with few questions asked if they went wrong.

By comparison the rigid airship was big and expensive and scarce. There was great moral, professional and financial pressure on the designer to get it right first time. Although the German Zeppelins were admired (and copied) by the British, they had been developed in twenty years mainly for war use, with an accident rate that could never have been accepted in peacetime. The designers of R.38, though basing their ideas on Zeppelin practice, aspired to do better. With the coming of peace they had their opportunity.

The Royal Airship Works was virtually created for R.38 and the future of lighter-than-air flight. It was a *centre of excellence* which aimed to focus all the best research available, similar to the Royal Aircraft Establishment at Farnborough. It had its own foundry, rolling mills, fabric shop, workshops and drawing office; admittedly much of it poached from Short Brothers. Expert workers were gathered in by cancelling airship orders to Vickers, Beardmore and Armstrong Whitworth. It had a lot going for it, but it suffered from the self-confidence which seems to make monopolies immune to advice and criticism.

It took the loss of R.38 to shatter this complacency. From this time on there was to be greater accountability in aeronautical matters, and not only *after* accidents, although the present scientific investigation of crashes has evolved from the Accidents Investigations Sub-Committee of 1921/22. Following their report, an Airships Stressing Panel was set up in 1922, comprising scientists who not only checked the designers' sums but also ensured that they were up to date on research. The powers of the Aeronautical Inspection Department (AID) were enhanced by the Air Navigation Order of 1922. In 1924 the Airworthiness of Airships Panel was set up as an Authority to control lighter-than-air flight. Much of this regulation, triggered by one spectacular disaster, came to be applied to all branches of aviation to the advantage of air travellers who may not enjoy the comfort and grace of airship flight, but who may now confidently hope to arrive safely.

If the lessons had been learned, what went wrong with Cardington built R.101, which crashed at Beauvais in October 1930 during a storm? Lessons learned are not necessarily lessons applied, and there is little doubt that the R.101 was dispatched on its fatal flight while it was still not fully tested and before its recurring nose-heaviness had been satisfactorily explained. For many years afterwards it was popularly believed that Secretary of State for Air Lord Thomson had forced the departure on 4 October 1930 for his own selfish and political motives. This is questioned in Sir Peter Masefield's definitive book on the R.101 disaster (*To Ride the Storm*, William Kimber, 1982) but the fact remains that some agency or circumstance forced a long proving flight on an unready ship against the judgement of responsible airshipmen. It is difficult to oppose the will of a powerful and charismatic employer - which, in effect, Lord

Thomson was to the airship community - and there would at least be a desire to please him.

There was also the momentum of public expectation which had been generated by years of government publicity about the coming glories of air travel. R.101 had been on a course of no return since its inception. Public opinion can be a merciless taskmaster, particularly if national pride is involved. Not only would R.101 (and R.100) wipe out the shame of R.38, but Germany's *Graf Zeppelin* was once more showing Britain up by successful trans-Atlantic flights. Unhappily, whereas blame may easily be apportioned to builders and fliers - the actual 'doers' - it is more difficult to make politicians accountable, and virtually impossible to indict the public in general.

Whatever forced the pace, the resulting loss of yet more brave and talented pioneers (48 deaths) finished British hopes for imperial airship communications. Apart from the brief flowering of the splendid Empire Flying Boats, it was to be twenty years before the *aeroplane* was ready to take over this task, but not yet with the grace and style of the giant passenger dirigible.

One very practical contribution of the big rigid was in the development of light alloy technology, which soon replaced wood in aircraft construction. Many aircraft builders learned their skills in the draughty halls of Cardington, Barrow, Barlow, or Inchinnan, and were available for the rapid expansion of metal construction in the 1930s and '40s.

By the time that the *Hindenburg* put a spectacular end to civil airship operations, the airship had pioneered long-distance passenger flight, had developed meteorology and pressure-pattern flying and had boosted navigation and radio communication - all to the benefit of Jet Age travellers.

In research and design, much more attention was now given to wind tunnel tests, in which models could cheaply, quickly and safely answer many questions which would be unfair to ask of men in the air. R.38 and its sisters had contributed to this science in the course of the National Physical Laboratory tests, which unfortunately killed Pannell and Duffield.

The annual competition for the R.38 Memorial Prize is still contributing to our understanding of aeronautics. The first winners were the American naval constructors Burgess, Hunsaker and Truscott, who presented a paper on 'The Strength of Rigid Airships'. They paid this tribute to the victims of R.38/ZR-2, which could serve to honour all experimenters who knowingly take risks in the pursuit of knowledge:

> The pioneers who lost their lives in R.38 made the
> crucial test of the state of our knowledge at that time.

We, who follow them, must proceed in all humility, and with full appreciation of the lessons which their splendid sacrifice has made available.

Le ceil fut son désir ——

Appendix A: Reappraisal of the Technical Evidence

The findings of the Accidents Investigation Sub-Committee of the Aeronautical Research Committee were published on 30 January 1922, just five months after the demise of R.38/ZR-2.

In their summary they attribute the loss to the structural weakness in the *design*, rather than faulty material or poor workmanship. They did not blame the handling, which had not imposed loads 'in excess of those which might have occurred during the normal navigation of the ship, in weather which might reasonably be encountered.' Thus they vindicated the builders, and also Pritchard and his colleagues who had made the apparently reckless decision to carry out the tests at low level.

Returning to the matter of design, they identified the following factors:

- the weakness of R.38 in relation to its size and speed;
- the accentuation of the weakness by the specially powerful control surfaces and the need to make 'large and rapid' movements to counteract the instability of the airship;
- reversals of such stressing conditions which 'may not improbably' have weakened the structure (i.e. *metal fatigue* in modern terms).

They criticised the designers' reliance on comparisons with existing ships (presumably the captured or downed Zeppelins and their British copies) instead of design and research by both model and full scale experiment. This was hardly fair to a dead Chief Designer whose team had slavishly calculated the weights and balancing moments and had co-operated fully with the test programme and the pressure measurements and wind tunnel calibration experiments by the NPL staff. However, they made the valid comment that the design team had decided to ignore known evidence from model experiments (indicating considerable aerodynamic forces on a model of R.29) on the grounds that R.29 had not broken up in flight. They further castigated Campbell and his team for failing to read or act upon existing research reports, or to call in expertise from outside the Royal Airship Works; (not specified, but by implication Pratt and Wallis of Vickers). As the Report carefully detailed the time scale for design and building, they might also decently have referred to the haste imposed by the Air Ministry to get the ship finished and off their hands.

In fairness, the Committee did admit that the requirements 'laid down in time of war were drastic and imposed too severe a task on the designers'.

The stricture which must still attach to the RAW design team was the *complete ignoring of aerodynamic forces*, on which there was sufficient published evidence to at least stimulate the imagination, and to suggest a more generous 'factor of ignorance' than the nominal 4 (actually found to be 1).

Possibly because this was a *technical* investigation, the Report contains no reference to the curtailment of the tests from 150 hours to a nominal 50; (the accident occurred after 56 hours due to the extension of the fourth flight). If this had been admitted as a main factor - as it undoubtedly was - the question of responsibility would have had to be faced, with inevitable embarrassment in high places and in the Committee, a number of whom were serving officers of the RAF and USN.

*   *   *

Setting aside the apportioning of blame, how did the ship break, burn and explode?

It is known that the girders were weak in compression due to (a) their lightness, (b) the unbraced length of the sections, and (c) the presence of intermittent lateral loads such as weights, vibration, local air pressure (e.g. propeller slipstream) and gas bag pressure. Campbell was fully aware of this and relied on the weights of the bow mooring gear and compensatory one-ton water ballast aft to keep the top longitudinals in tension, while the lower members, reinforced by the keel walkway, would remain in compression. In engineering terms, it was a *hogging* condition, with a tendency to make the ends sag in level flight. During manoeuvring, or even hunting about a mean course or altitude, these stresses would increase and decrease, perhaps even to the point of *reversal*.

In straight flight, the flank longitudinals (e.g. D girders) would in theory be neutrally stressed, but would suffer alternate tensions and compressions during turning or hunting. Those main and intermediate girders between top and bottom (e.g. A' to C', D' to F') would have complex loads due to 'working' of the framework in the vertical and horizontal planes. This would be further complicated by the variable presence of fuel, ballast and crew, and by the *oblique* thrust wires from the engines attached to the framework at joints between rings and longitudinals. With the engines - particularly the midships pair - placed so far off centre due to the height limitations in the construction shed (later raised for R.101), these wires would have imposed considerable local compressive forces, especially during turning.

It is reasonable to guess that the break-up, which occurred obliquely between Frames 9 and 10, commenced with the collapse of some of the lower flank longitudinal girders aft of the starboard rear engine car at Frame 9, from which the straining wire ran back to E11 (longitudinal E, Frame 11). The buckling would then have spread upwards, causing the puckering effect noticed by witnesses, most of whom reported that the ends of the ship first sagged before the final severance.

Further evidence of an initial *compressive* collapse is given by the sudden veering to starboard, suggesting that the hull had jack-knifed before parting.

*   *   *

The cause of the fire was a source of speculation in the absence of witnesses who would have been in the keel at the time. The Court of Inquiry (and the Accidents Investigation Sub-Committee) concluded that a petrol pipe and an electrical lead had been severed in proximity, and that a spark from a short-circuit had ignited the fuel. Later (too late to be included in the Committee's report) experiments conducted at Cardington by Flight Lieutenant H. Cooch failed to ignite petrol close to a number of test breaks of an electric circuit. Care was taken to set up circuits similar to those in R.38, but it was only after simulating intermittent sparking, such as would be caused by a broken cable being pulled through a conduit, that ignition occurred before the protective fuse blew. In the light of accumulated knowledge of aeronautical design - and misadventure - since that time, it seems possible that the experimenters underestimated two factors:

(a)   that the extreme turbulence round a broken airship travelling at 50-plus knots would rapidly vaporise petrol and mix it with air to an ignitable state;

(b)   not only the interruption of an *inductive circuit* would tend to produce an arc rather than a mere spark. (The author had the

Copy of Instructions
Issued 5th July to C.O. Ship
& 23rd July to C.O. Ship
& to Comd Maxfield
on 17th Aug. 1921

R.38.

1. All disposable weights in the corridor should be situated as near the main frames as possible. No heavy weights should be placed between the adjacent intermediate frames.

2. Concentrated weights of more than 300 lbs should not be hung from the box girders in the corridor except at the joints of the side keel struts.

3. To avoid undue bending moments and shearing forces on the hull structure, the attached diagram showing the distribution of disposable weights corresponding toe various percentage fullness of the gasbags at ground level, should be worked to as nearly as possible. The ordinates of the curves represents the total disposable weight allowable over the frame space.

4. In general, the petrol between Frames 5 and 9 should be used when the ship has lift corresponding to more than 90% of the lift at ground level. Below 90%, petrol at the ends of the ship should beused in preference to the petrol carried amidships. The total disposable weight over any frame space should agree as nearly as possible with the distribution shown on the attached chart. This precaution enables the ship's structure to be kept on a hogging condition under all variations of buoyancy.

5. The bulk of food and fresh water for long patrols should preferably be stowed in way of, and alternative to, the existing water ballast stowage to prevent undue loading of the corridor.

6. Weights in the crew spaces should be kept as low as possible: not more than 15 persons should be allowed in the crew space at any time.

7. With the ship having a lift corresponding to 70% of the lift at ground level, not more than two of the fixed petrol tanks at Frames 5, 7 and 9 should be full.

8. When bombs are carried, the amount of fixed petrol at Frames 5, 7 and 9 should be reduced by an amount corresponding to the weight of the bombs.

9. Corresponding port and starboard tanks should be emptied in turn, thus avoiding having two petrol tanks full on one side, with the opposite tanks empty in any particular space.

10. Emergency water ballast in the vicinity of Frame 7 should only be carried alternative to bombs. Paragraph 8 applies in the case of ballast being carried alternative to bombs.

11. Not more than seven people should be allowed in the control car space at any time.

12. Under normal conditions not more than four persons should be allowed abaft Frame 13, and not more than two abaft Frame 15. With the ship in a condition of lift less than 70% of the lift at ground level, only two persons should be allowed abaft Frame 13, and not more than one abaft Frame 15.

13. With the pair emergency water ballast bags at Frame 1 full, only two of the bags at Frame 2 should be full, thus limiting the emergency water ballast at the forward end of the ship to 2,500 lbs.

14. Difference of pressure in adjacent gasbags of more than 5 mm of water should be avoided. This applies particularly to gasbags 3 to 12 inclusive.

15. In the case of a deflated gasbag, all disposable weights should be jettisoned at the main frames bounding the gasbag and the adjacent gasbags should be deflated to 75% full.

16. In general, not more than three persons should be allowed in an engine car at the same time.

17. Not more than two persons should be allowed on any five metre length of the corridor walking way girder at the same time.

18. When flying at a speed of 50 knots, a height of 2,000 to 3000 feet above the ground should be maintained. Correspondingly higher altitudes should be maintained at higher speeds than this.

Fig. 88 Facsimile of the restrictive loading instructions given to Commander Maxfield only one week before the final flight.

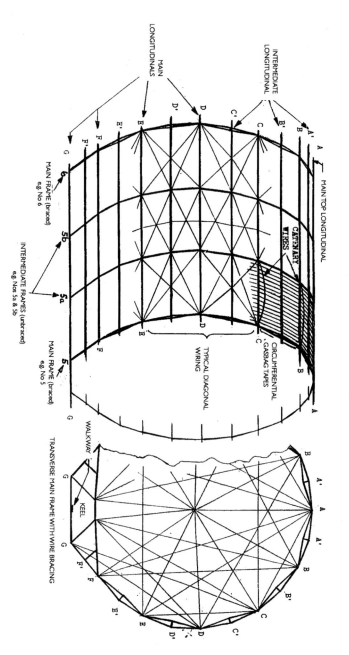

TYPICAL 45 metre BAY WITH TWO UNBRACED INTERMEDIATE FRAMES.
THE FRAMES ARE DESIGNATED NUMBERS AND THE LONGITUDINALS
BY LETTERS. MAIN FRAME AND DIAGONAL WIRE BRACING IS SHOWN;
ALSO THE CIRCUMFERENTIAL GASBAG SUPPORT TAPES AND CATENARY WIRES

MAIN TOP LONGITUDINAL

MAIN
LONGITUDINALS

INTERMEDIATE
LONGITUDINAL

CATENARY
WIRES

MAIN FRAME (braced)
e.g. No 6

INTERMEDIATE FRAMES (unbraced)
e.g. Nos 5a & 5b

MAIN FRAME (braced)
e.g. No 5

TYPICAL DIAGONAL
WIRING

CIRCUMFERENTIAL
GASBAG TAPES

TRANSVERSE MAIN FRAME WITH WIRE BRACING

WALKWAY

KEEL

Fig. 89 Typical 45-metre bay with two intermediate frames. The frames are designated by numbers and the longitudinals by letters. Main frame and diagonal wire bracing is shown; also the circumferential gasbag support tapes and catenary wires.

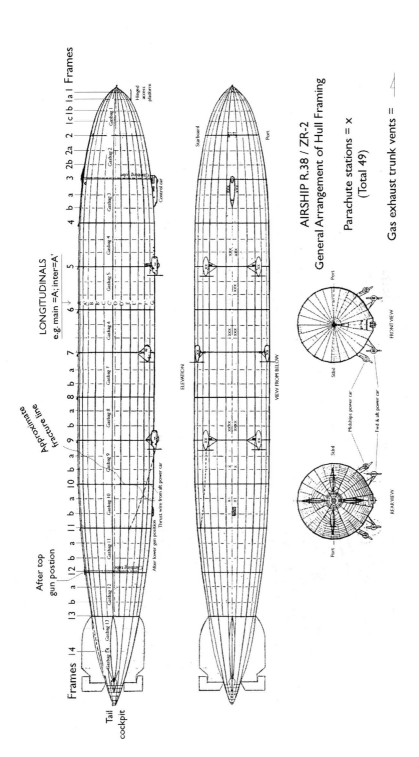

Fig. 90 Airship R.38/ZR-2 - General arrangement of Hull framing.

Fig. 91 The wireless installation in R.34, similar to R.38's equipment.

Fig. 92 Switch and fuse panel in one of R.38's engine cars.

Fig. 93 The ripples in the envelope of R.100 show the presence of turbulence around an airship. This probably contributed to the explosion of the hydrogen from R.38's ruptured cells.

educational experience of creating a most spectacular arc as a student engineer by breaking a connection during the laboratory test of a D.C. generator.)

Flight Lieutenant Cooch's team assumed that the airship's 12 volt battery, in parallel with a generator, 'would constitute a practically non-inductive circuit' - by its nature not prone to arcing. In theory, perhaps; but a dynamo driven by a main engine (the port after Cossack), and therefore unable to stall, is unhappy about short circuits and is capable of sending sizeable sparks across the flailing ends of broken wires. This might possibly be accentuated by the presence of relays in any of the circuits affected, e.g. horn and telephone relays; and it is not certain that only the lighting circuits *aft* of the generator were broken. It is feasible that the separation could have *pulled* wires apart *forward* of the hull fracture, which occurred between Frames 9 and 10. A simple fuse requires a sufficient current for a substantial fraction of a second before melting, and intermittent sparking would be unlikely to trigger it. A very small spark can ignite a critical mixture of petrol vapour and air.

Whatever the cause, the potential hazard of petrol in airships was to haunt future designers, to the extent of condemning R.101 to the burden of heavy and untried diesel engines for its proposed tropical service.

The explosions which followed the fire in the fore part of R.38 were nothing like the often televised burning of the German airship *Hindenburg* at Lakehurst, N.J., in 1937. By contrast, the hydrogen gas of R.38/ZR-2 exploded twice, with massive detonations which broke windows in Hull and which were felt many miles away. This can only have been possible by the rupturing of some gas cells while the ship was still in motion and surrounded by turbulence, giving an instant mix of gas and air to critically explosive proportion. Hydrogen will only burn in contact with air, and will not *explode* until the mixture is right.

In the 1970s a scientist employed by a chemical company visited Hull to enquire about the R.38 explosion in the course of a pre-emptive investigation into the conditions for a gas-air explosion. He was shown photographs of R.100 at speed, with ripples in the canvas cover indicating turbulence, to support the 'critical mix' theory.

In 1974, on the south bank of the Humber and not many miles from the R.38 explosion, a leak at the Flixborough chemical plant caused a slow accumulation of gas into sheltered air between some buildings. When the proportions were right, something detonated the mixture. The bang was heard in Hull. 29 people died.

Appendix B: The Howden Detachment

The United States Naval Rigid Airship Detachment

The Detachment arrived at the Royal Air Force Base, Howden, East Yorkshire on 20 April 1920. It consisted of the following officers and enlisted personnel († Died in crash, * Survived):

Commander L H Maxfield,	†	Washington, DC.	Commanding
Lieut Comdr V N Bieg,	†	Bryn Mawr, Pa.	Chief Engineer
Lieut Comdr R G Pennoyer		Berkeley, Calif.	Executive Officer
Lieut C G Little	†	Newburyport, Mass	
Lieut T B Null		Ruffsdale, Pa	
Lieut J B Lawrence		Lincoln, Minn.	
Lieut A R Houghton			
Lieut W R Taylor			Medical Officer
Lieut (jg) J H Kyger			Supply Officer
CBM C I Aller	†	Denver, Col.	
CQM A E Carlson		Juliaetta, Idaho	
CQM H Cristensen		Newton, Mass.	
CMM R M Coons	†	Owensboro, Ky	
CMM J W Cullinan		Binghamton, NY	
CMM A B Galatian		New York City	
CMM J T Hancock	†	London, Eng	
CQM J J Harrigan			
CMM W A Julius	†	Los Angeles	
CBM M Lay	†	Greensboro, N.C.	
CBM H H O'Claire			
CBM A D Pettit	†	New York City	
CMM W A Russell		Brooklyn, NY	
CMM L T Stephens		Atlanta, Ga	
CMM W J Steele	†	Bainbridge, Ind	
CQM T L Thomas		Anderson, S Carolina	
CMM F M Gorey		New York City	
QM1 S H Knight		Philadelphia, Pa	

In July 1920 a second draft of officers and enlisted men 'reported aboard' at Howden:

Lieut Comdr E W Coil	†	Marietta, Ohio
Lieut F P Culbert		
Lieut H W Hoyt	†	Clearwater, Fla
Lieut M H Esterly	†	Washington DC
Ensign W J Medusky		
Ensign J H Hykes		

CM S S Halliburton		Macon, Ga
CMM C H Broom		Atlantic City, NJ
CMM L K Coleman		Fort Worth, Texas
CCM J H Collier		Oklahoma City
CMM L E Crowl	†	S Carolina
MM1 C M Deem		
QM1 C W Frank		Waynoka, Okla
QM1 C A Heckbert		Rockland, Maine
MM1 R Jones		Los Angeles, Calif
CQM J J Leonard		
CQM E C Lewis		
CMMA L Loftin	†	
MM1 C J McCarthy		
CQM F L Peckham		
CCM S F Shields		St Louis, Mo
E1 J E Waterman		El Paso, Texas
QM1 N O Walker	*	Commerce, Texas
CMM G Welch	†	Elgin, Ill
CMM F F Moorman		St Louis, Mo

The following reported at various intervals:

Lieut J B Anderson	Hyattsville, Md	Met Officer
CMM T D Dickerson	Summerland, Calif	
CMM W A Lamkey	Brooklyn, NY	
CMM C W Cass	Jacksonville, Fla	
FPM E S Downs		
CY E M Riley		
CE J T Robertson	New Smyrna, Fla	
E3 F Kuback		
Y2 F H Cutler		
Y3 M C Hegel		
MM1 S Solar		

Source: Smithsonian Institution / US Naval Historical Center

The British Crew on the Final Flight

Royal Air Force
Air Commodore E M Maitland, CMG DSO AFC   †
Flt Lt J E M Pritchard, OBE AFC (Air Ministry representative)   †
Flt Lt I C Little, AFC   †
Flt Lt R S Montagu, DSC (Navigator)   †
Flt Lt G M Thomas, DFC   †
Flt Lt A H Wann, AFC (Captain)   *
Flying Officer T F Matthewson, AFC (Engineer Officer)   †
Flying Officer V H Wicks (Wireless Officer)   †

Flgy Sgt W H Greener	†	LAC G S Anger	†
Flt Sgt S J Heath	†	LAC W Oliver	†
Flt Sgt A T Martin	†	LAC J N Wilson	†
Flt Sgt J Rye	†	AC1 E W Davies	*
Flt Sgt F Smith	†	AC1 C W Donald	†
Flt Sgt H Thompson	†	AC1 J O Drew	†
Sgt F E Burton	†	AC2 R Parker	†
Sgt J W Mason	†	AC1 C W Penson	†
		AC1 E E Steere	†
		AC2 R Withington	†

Cpl W Potter   *

National Physical Laboratory
H Batement   *
C W Duffield   †
J R Pannell   †

Royal Airship Works
C I R Campbell   †
F Warren   †

BIBLIOGRAPHY

Abbott, Patrick, *Airship The Story of R.34* (Adams & Dart, 1973), New edition, (Brewin Books, Studley, Warwickshire, 1994).

Abbott, Patrick, *The British Airship at War, 1914-1918* (Terence Dalton, 1989).

Allen, Peter, *The 91 before Lindberg* (Airlife Publishing Ltd, 1984).

Beaubois, Henry, *Airships* (Macdonald & Jane's, 1974).

Botting, Douglas, *The Giant Airships* (Time-Life Books, 1981).

Burney, Sir Dennis, *The World, The Air and the Future* (Alfred A. Knopf, 1929).

Von Buttlar, Treusch, *Zeppelins over England* (Harrap, 1931).

Chamberlain, Geoffrey, *Airships - Cardington* (Terence Dalton, 1984).

Clausberg, Karl, *Zeppelin,* (German text) (Schirmer-Mosel, 1979).

Collier, Basil, *The Airship* (Hart-Davis, MacGibbon, 1974).

Connon, Peter, *An Aeronautical History of the Cumbria, Dumfries and Galloway Region, Pt. 2: 1915 to 1930* (St. Patrick;'s Press, Penrith, 1984).

Dean, Christopher, (Ed.) *Housing the Airship* (Architectural Association, 1989).

Dodsworth, Ted, *Wings over Yorkshire* (Hutton Press, 1988).

Duval, G.R. *War in the Air 1914-1918* (D. Bradford Barton, Truro, 1975).

Gamble, C.T. Snowdon, *The Story of a North Sea Air Station* (Oxford University Press, 1928).

Hartcup, Guy, *The Achievement of the Airship* (David & Charles, 1974).

Higham, Robert, *The British Airship* (Foulis, 1961).

Horton, Edward, *The Age of the Airship* (Sidgwick & Jackson, 1973).

Kinsey, Gordon, *Pulham Pigs* (Terence Dalton, 1988).

Leasor, James, *The Millionth Chance* (Hamish Hamilton, 1957).

Liddle, Peter H. *The Sailor's War 1914-1918* (Blandford, 1985).

Longstaff, Reginald, *The Fleet Air Arm, a Pictorial History* (Robert Hale,1981).

Maitland, E.M. *The Log of H.M.A. R.34: Journey to America and Back,* (Hodder & Stoughton, 1921).

Masefield, Sir Peter G. *To Ride the Storm* (William Kimber, 1982).

Morpurgo, J.E. *Barnes Wallis* (Longman, 1972).

Pratt, H.B. *Commercial Airships* (Nelson, 1920).

Rimell, Raymond L. *Air War over Great Britain 1914-1918* (Arms & Armour Press, 1987).

Robinson, Douglas H. *The Zeppelin in Combat,* 2nd ed. rev. 1966 (Foulis, 1962).

Shute, Nevil, *Slide Rule* (William Heinemann, 1954).

Sinclair, J.A. *Airships in Peace and War* (Rich & Cowan, 1934).

Toland, John, *Ships in the Sky* (Frederick Muller, 1957).

Van der Vat, Dan, *The Atlantic Campaign 1939-45, (includes chapter on WW1)* (Hodder & Stoughton, 1988).

Ventry, Lord & Kolesnik, Eugene M. *Airship Saga* (Blandford Press, 1982).

Whitehouse, Arch. *The Zeppelin Fighters* (Robert Hale, 1968).

Williams, T.B. *Airship Pilot No. 28* (William Kimber, 1974).

INDEX

Index